S0-DTC-371

Thomas
AQUINAS

PROVIDENCE
AND PREDESTINATION

TRUTH, Questions 5 & 6

Translated from the definitive Leonine
text and with an
Introduction by
Robert W. Mulligan, S.J., Ph.D.

Regnery/Gateway, Inc.
South Bend, Indiana

International Standard Book Number: 0-89526-937-6

CONTENTS

PREDESTINATION

Introduction

I

St. Thomas: His Life and General Teachings

The first half of the thirteenth century was marked by the first use of pagan literature in western European philosophical thought. Although Toledo was re-conquered from the Moors in 1085, it was only gradually that this small city assumed enormous importance as one of the principal points of encounter between the Christian world and the Moslem world. Its Jewish and Arabian population furnished indispensable help for the translation into Latin of scientific writings by Aristotle and by such Arabian geniuses as Avicenna (980-1037) and Averroes (1126-1198). It was, however, the indomitable energy of Toledo's bishop, Dominicus Gundissalinus (d. 1151), that directed much of the work of translating and of introducing the riches of Greek and Arabian philosophy to the new schools of the Christian West.

Scholars trained in Toledo often came to Naples to the court of Emperor Frederic II (1197-1250), who invited philosophers of every culture and creed. Thus in 1227, Michael Scot joined the imperial court, coming from Toledo where he had translated several writings of Aristotle and some of the commentaries on Aristotle composed by Avicenna. In Naples, too, Scot undertook a Latin translation of the writings of Averroes. In short, during the reign of Frederick and of his bastard son Manfred (1258-1266) Naples was a center of intellectual activity. It was stirred deeply by the introduction of Greek thought and Arabian philosophy, and it would have been strange if Thomas Aquinas had been unaffected when he studied there as a youth.

St. Thomas was born in 1225, at Roccasecca, not far from Naples, and he received his early education at the Benedictine monastery of Monte Cassino, the cradle of the Benedictine Order, eighty miles south of Rome. From 1239 to 1244, however, he studied at the University of Naples, where he probably made his first acquaintanceship with the writings of Aristotle, as well as with those of the Arabian philosophers, Avicenna and Averroes, whom he quotes extensively in his own writings of later years.

The date of his entry into the Order of St. Dominic is not known, but it seems that he studied philosophy under St. Albert the Great in Paris before 1248, and certainly later between 1248 and 1252. In 1252, Thomas began his theological studies in Paris, and after three years obtained a degree entitling him to teach in the University.

Called to Italy in 1259, Thomas spent the next ten years as a member of the papal court where he taught theology as part of his duties. During this time, he became close friends with a distinguished Flemish scholar and fellow Dominican, William Moerbeke, whose knowledge of Greek enabled Thomas, who knew very little, to undertake a series of commentaries on the writings of Aristotle.

In 1269, Thomas returned to Paris and resumed his teaching career. The university circles in Paris were in turmoil. The growing popularity of Aristotle was regarded with suspicion by conservatives, who pointed out that many of Aristotle's teachings were in open conflict with the Christian faith. He holds, for example, that the world is eternal and uncreated. Moreover, instead of speaking of one God, he speaks of fifty-five unmoved movers in the Metaphysics. His writings, especially as interpreted by Averroes and Avicenna, seem even to exclude divine providence and personal immortality. In the eyes of the authorities, the writings of St. Augustine, profound and pious, seemed vastly preferable as teaching material to the profane writings of a pagan which would seem to endanger the faith of the young students.

Unfortunately, some extremists advocating Aristotle had tried to establish a double standard of truth whereby a doctrine such as the personal immortality of the soul could be held philosophically false but theologically true. They ascribed their double standard theory to Aver-roes. Others used this quarrel as an occasion to protest against monks teaching in the uni-versity at all.

Serenely confident that there could be no conflict between his faith and his intelligence, Thomas sided with the Aristotelians. Although profoundly respectful toward the writings of St. Augustine, he did not hesitate to criticize Augus-tine and to speak of his theories as being "satu-rated with Platonism." To the scandal of some of his contemporaries, he admitted that he could not demonstrate that the world was not eternal. Absolutely speaking, Thomas wrote, God could have kept the world in existence from all eternity. Only from faith does the Christian know that the world has a limited age.

Again, he dismissed the ontological argument for the existence of God popularized by St. Anselm, and in opposition to St. Augustine held that government is not a result of man's sinful nature but rather an instrument to aid the com-mon good which would be necessary even if man had never fallen from his original state of grace. Like his teacher, St. Albert the Great, Thomas quoted extensively and approvingly from the writings of both the Church Fathers and Mo-hammedan philosophers. One of his favorite authors seems to have been a rabbi, Moses Maimonides, whose arguments Thomas cites fre-quently and rarely criticizes. In short, Thomas gave such abundant evidence of intellectual honesty that when he did criticize other philosophers, his arguments were viewed with respect even when they were not accepted.

As noted earlier, two of the philosophers whom Thomas cites frequently are Avicenna and Averroes. The former, sometimes known as Ibn Sina, was born near Bokhara in Persia, and is regarded even today by many as the greatest mind ever produced by the Moslem world. His principal work was the *As-Sifa*, which comprised logic, physics, mathematics, philosophical psychology, and metaphysics, and his teaching on the distinction between essence and existence in created things deeply influenced St. Thomas. Averroes or Ibn Rusd, another great disciple of Aristotle, was born in Cordoba, Spain, in 1126 while it was still under Moorish domination. Although St. Thomas regarded Averroes as one of the great authorities on the teaching of Aristotle, he was highly critical of his position which excluded personal survival after death. In this, however, Averroes was probably more faithful to the teaching of Aristotle than was St. Thomas, who thought he could find passages and principles in Aristotle supporting personal immortality.

It might be mentioned in passing, that both Avicenna and Averroes failed to recognize that a work called *The Elements of Theology* was not a work of Aristotle, but actually consisted of extracts from the *Enneads* of Plotinus (204-270 A.D.), a neo-Platonist. The Platonic teachings in this work considerably distorted the interpretations which both Avicenna and Averroes made of Aristotle's system, and St. Thomas often found himself in the difficult position of defending Aristotle from the Aristotelians.

As early as 1210 an ecclesiastical council in Paris had forbidden the teaching of Aristotle, and even though this interdiction was lifted by the time that St. Thomas began his teaching career, still the task which he took upon himself of reconciling the wisdom of the Greeks with the revelations of Christianity was a very heavy one. Without openly criticizing conservative thinkers such as Alexander of Hales and St. Bonaventure whose works continued the Augustinian tradition, St. Thomas began to construct a system that was based far more on Aristotle's empiricism than on the Platonic idealism latent in the writings of St. Augustine.

Thomas insisted, for example, that all human knowledge must originate in sense experience. He excludes divine illumination from normal human intellection, and argues that even knowledge of the existence of God is derived by reasoning from evidence around us, rather than from an idea or light within us. The immediate object of the human intellect, Thomas teaches, is the essence of material things. In its first operation, the mind attains a thing in its essence. In its second, which is the judgment, the intellect attains the object of its act of being. Unlike those who in the spirit of Plato conceive of truth as the understanding of essences, St.

Thomas holds that truth is related more to knowing a thing in its act of being rather than in its quiddity, for a true judgment is one whereby we have intellectually grasped the essence of a thing as it exists in reality. Knowledge of God exists as the peak of this philosophy, and the normal way to reach such knowledge is by reflecting upon the meaning of the vast universe around us and the concrete conditions necessary for its existence.

To grasp the spirit of St. Thomas, then, one must think of him as a young intellectual raised in a conservative tradition, but deeply moved by the discoveries of Greek and Arabian philosophy and serenely confident of Christianity's ability to assimilate them, despite the fears and hesitations of his contemporaries.

It must not be thought, however, that St. Thomas simply inserted the philosophy of Aristotle into his own. St. Thomas retained many elements of Augustinianism, and borrowed extensively from Pseudo-Dionysius, from the neo-Platonist Proclus and from others such as Avicenna, Averroes, and Moses Maimonides. Many of his key teachings, however, were taken from Aristotle, and to him his debt is greatest. Thus, the Aristotelian principle of the distinction between potency and act is operative throughout all of Thomas' writings; but he extended this distinction which in Aristotle is largely confined to the levels of substance and accident to apply also to the distinction between the quiddity of a finite thing and its act of existence. This distinction is already found in authors such as Avicenna, and the writings of Avicenna may have been the source of his original inspiration. But no one had employed the distinction as widely as Thomas did. It enabled him, for example, to go beyond the unmoved movers which Aristotle had established to explain the existence of motion, and to argue to a unique and infinite being, whose continuing activity was necessary to keep contingent beings in existence. This distinction also enabled him to defend the meaningfulness of arguments for the existence of God that are based on the nature of being, because the principles and terms describing being are valid for all, both finite and infinite beings. Finally, by conceiving any determinate essence as a limitation of being and removing this limitation upon the divine nature by affirming that in God essence and existence are identical, Thomas avoided the anthropomorphism which conceives of infinity as including all beings, rather than as containing all perfections.

St. Thomas also developed Aristotle's teaching on the relationship between the soul and the body. In his earlier works, Aristotle speaks of the soul as though it were localized in the heart—somewhat as Descartes localized it in the pineal gland of the brain. In his later works, however, Aristotle describes the soul as the "entelechy" or energy and action of the entire body. "If the eye were an independent animal," he writes, "its soul would be sight." He thus conceives the soul not as a structure but as the source of man's total energy—his life force. The soul is that which makes a body to be a living body. In this view, accepted by St. Thomas, the soul and body are not two complete beings, each with its own existence, joined in a loose union, as some Platonists held. They are two incomplete substances, the body sharing the existence belonging to the soul, the two together constituting one human being.

In Aristotle, however, the person as such is perishable. Upon its dissolution from the body, the soul loses that which made it distinct and individual. As a consequence, it is somehow absorbed by a higher spiritual force whose characteristics Aristotle does not describe. St. Thomas rejects Aristotle's view here, and maintains that since the soul is a being whose activities are not restricted to animating a body, when the body can no longer share the existence which it derives from the soul, the soul can continue in existence apart from it. It will not be absorbed into any "over-soul" inasmuch as its individuality is rooted in its existence, which is incommunicable and unique. Such a concept of the human soul as an intellectual substance having its own act of existence apart from its individuating relationship with a body is not to be found in the writings of Aristotle, and it is precisely that which enabled Thomas to answer the problem of personal immortality.

There are other differences between Aristotle and St. Thomas. The God of Aristotle's *Metaphysics* is loved by all beings, moves all beings, but does not create any being. The God of Aristotle is wrapped up in sublime self-contemplation, for only an infinite object is proper for an infinite intellect; and although St. Thomas argued that it does not follow that things other than God would be unknown to Him if He knew Himself, for by knowing Himself He knows all things, this explanation was far more appropriate to Thomas' own philosophical system which affirmed that God keeps all beings in existence by continued causal activity than it was to Aristotle's system which describes the world as eternal and self-explanatory. It is true that Aristotle speaks of unmoved movers affecting the different spheres of the universe, but there is literally an infinite distance between the movers of the heavenly spheres and the unique Being whose love—to use Dante's phrase—moves all.

The second period of St. Thomas in Paris lasted only three years. In 1272, he was recalled to Italy by his religious superiors to organize a program of theological studies in Naples. Asked to participate in an ecumenical council held at Lyons, France, in 1274, St. Thomas fell ill en route or—according to another tradition—was injured by a low hanging branch of a tree. Carried to a monastery at Fosesanova, Italy, he died on the seventh day of March at the age of forty-nine.

On March 7, 1277, exactly three years after the death of St. Thomas, the quarrels between rationalistic Aristotelians led by Siger of Brabant (1235-1282) and the conservative Augustinians came to a climax when Stephen Tempier, Bishop of Paris, condemned two hundred and nineteen propositions currently being taught in Paris. This decree is worth mentioning since it included a number of doctrines openly professed by St. Thomas. But a year after the Paris condemnation, a general chapter of the Dominican Order held in Milan declared that the teachings of Thomas Aquinas were the official doctrine of the Order, and in 1323, Aquinas was recognized as a saint by the Catholic Church.

In general, the study of St. Thomas followed the lines and the fortunes of philosophical thought. As medieval scholasticism declined in vigor, the study of St. Thomas dwindled, and its rich intuitions went unused. At the end of the nineteenth century, Pope Leo XIII issued an encyclical or official document, assigning a privileged place to the study of St. Thomas in Catholic seminaries and universities. Although the study of other philosophers and theologians was by no means excluded, still this directive that special attention be given to the study of St. Thomas resulted in a vigorous revival of Thomism which is still continuing both here and abroad, and the relevance of his writings to modern times is acknowledged by distinguished thinkers, Catholic, Protestant, and Jewish.

II

The Disputed Questions on Providence and Predestination

In medieval universities, it was customary for professors of philosophy and theology to hold public debates frequently throughout the academic year. These debates were known as "quaestiones disputatae"; and these "quaestiones disputatae" concerning the nature of truth were apparently held at the University of Paris under the direction of St. Thomas during three academic years 1256-57, 1257-58, and 1258-59. Twenty-nine questions or topics are treated in the entire work. The first twenty questions deal with the nature and forms of truth. The last questions treat the will; and even though they consider such matters as divine grace and Christ (its cause and source), still the debate is centered about the operation of the human will, its judgments and desires.

Truth represents the thought of St. Thomas himself, although the volume arose out of the public debates described above, which primarily involved students working under St. Thomas's direction. As already mentioned, while St. Thomas was teaching theology at Paris, it was customary to appoint young scholars to defend some position or to discuss some problem that was chosen in advance by his professor. On the day of the debate, classes assembled in a great hall. A young scholar would outline a problem and take a position, answering objections and arguments raised by those in the audience. On the following day, the professor in charge would give an oral report of the debate, summarize what had taken place, and would then give his own views.

The present work contains, then, St. Thomas's own summary of more than 250 public debates, together with his own teaching on the problems discussed. Each article usually begins with a list of arguments constituting the grounds of opposition to the view that he himself will hold and will describe in the *corpus* or body of the article, called "the reply." Immediately before the reply are listed arguments "to the contrary" i.e., arguments opposing those that have just been cited. Although these normally support the position of St. Thomas they are not to be taken as his own, for frequently he is merely citing arguments proposed by the young disputant or by those present at the public debate. The reply is followed by answers to the objections that were raised initially. At times a series of statements is appended to the answers, discussing or replying to the arguments proposed by those in the audience in favor of the basic position. But this happens only when St. Thomas feels that such arguments, although favorable to his views, are nevertheless deficient as they stand.

The seemingly clumsy mechanics of the debates are often irritating to the impatient, and many, feeling that they lose little by omitting the initial difficulties listed in each article, prefer to read the reply without having read the difficulties. This procedure will in some instances result in misunderstanding, for the difficulties furnish the context of the argument, and it is only too easy to misunderstand the entire meaning of an argument outside of the context from which it has arisen. In other words, the difficulties shape the question. They constitute the problematic. Although St. Thomas usually goes far beyond the problems proposed, to omit reading the difficulties entirely involves missing the dialectical origins of his thought and risks misunderstanding the position which he ultimately takes.

The present volume begins with the fifth question treated in the debates of 1256-59—the question of divine providence. Always an agonizing problem, it was particularly pressing in the time of St. Thomas inasmuch as the philosophy of Aristotle, newly introduced into medieval intellectual life, apparently excluded divine knowledge of creatures. As noted earlier, Aristotle argued that the proportioned object of the divine intellect must itself be divine, and this excludes knowledge of anything other than the divine essence. Moreover, in the neo-Platonic school of thought, represented by the writings of such geniuses as Avicenna, divine providence and care over creatures was excluded, inasmuch as Avicenna argued that knowledge involves duality (of subject and object), and there can be neither duality of essence and existence nor duality of knowledge in the supreme being. What providence there is—according to Avicenna— must be exercised by an intelligence issuing from God but inferior to Him.

The dilemma was simple: if God is infinite, He knows only His own infinite essence and nothing else. If He is not infinite, He is not God. Hence, if God is God, there is no providence. St. Thomas resolves the dilemma by pointing out that by knowing His own infinite essence God knows all beings; and like Aristotle before him and Hegel who comes much later, St. Thomas demonstrated that the act of knowledge does not necessarily imply duality of subject and object.

Infinite providence, however, does not mean an arbitrary providence to St. Thomas. Hence in the very first article of the question dealing with the divine plan or providence he excludes the views of those who held that divine providence is simply a matter of God's good pleasure, unfathomable because irrational. He insists that God's providence, however mysterious, is intelligent and involves His understanding. Yet it is not limited to the passive knowledge of a spectator. God has created the world for the highest possible purpose, namely, that it should manifest the divine goodness and, in the case of man, that he should possess it through that vision of God known as beatitude. The divine plan to carry out this purpose is divine providence, and involves both God's knowledge and His will. Since this plan is based upon His understanding of His own essence, providence cannot be arbitrary or irrational. Since His plan is based upon love—love of His own goodness and all that reflects it—His providence includes the divine will as it selects the final end of creation and the means whereby it can be obtained.

In the second article of the question treating providence, several key objections are raised. First of all, a neo-Platonic argument is described which alleges that as God is absolute Goodness, He necessarily tends to give from His Goodness, and this means that He creates necessarily. Moreover, since God is a necessary being, He must necessarily be a creator, since all the attributes of a necessary being must also be necessary. Thus divine liberty is excluded, and God's planning becomes not free but forced. Aristotelians raised another argument. Since the universe is constituted by countless beings, each obeying the inner dynamisms of its nature, any divine plan other than the original plan of creation would be useless, since the workings of the universe, once created, are fixed forever. Thus God stands helpless, confronted by His handiwork.

In his reply, St. Thomas almost seems to combine the neo-Platonic vision of goodness as immanent within the universe with the Aristotelian concept of natural causes. Arguing as Aristotle had done from our experience of a general order in the universe whose operations are so regular that they can be predicted almost infallibly, Thomas avers that this order cannot be the effect of chance. To say that an intelligible, articulated order arises somehow from chance and disorder is simply to re-state the problem. It does not solve it. Since the beings themselves that constitute this order are without intelligence, there must be some other being, highly intelligent, which directs each being in nature to its own end in such a manner that by achieving its own end it also becomes a part of a vast complexus, the universe, whose orderly splendor staggers the intellect. Such order can be found in the eye. Each of the intricate parts of the eye, by achieving its own purpose according to the dynamics of its own nature, contributes to a large purpose, the act of vision. Thus the universe arises like a symphony. Each musician plays only what is set before him on the score. Taken by itself, what each man plays is almost meaningless. Taken together, the swelling sounds of the instruments are easily recognizable as Beethoven's Third Symphony. The total symphony is not explicable either through chance or through the action of each player in isolation. It arises from each musician fulfilling his own role as correlated with a larger purpose and plan.

Throughout this section, St. Thomas emphasizes the continuing function of divine providence by pointing out that all God has brought into existence He can also reduce to nothingness, because the creative action of God must be a constant function. Without it, creatures would lapse back into nothingness. The creative activity of God, St. Thomas writes, "must not be compared with the action of a carpenter building a house, for, when his action ceases, the house still remains; it should rather be compared to the sun's lighting up the air." When the sun ceases its action, light immediately disappears. "Consequently, when God no longer gives existence to a creature whose very existence depends upon His will, then the creature is reduced to nothingness." God is in no sense then helpless before His handiwork.

As the debate over God's providence continues, St. Thomas treats other problems that were and are still current. One issue centered around God's providence over corruptible beings. In the view of the Aristotelians, the sole object of the divine knowledge was the divine essence, infinite power. They also argued that no spiritual being, such as God, could have knowledge of individual, material beings inasmuch as matter, upon which individual differences are based, is by nature intelligible, and no one can deduce the constituent characteristics of a particular person from this general notion of man. Following the line of this argument, certain contemporaries of St. Thomas argued that this kind of providence would be sufficient for animals and lower creatures, for divine provision could be made at least for the species represented by the general notion. Since the maintenance of only the species is of prime importance as regards material beings other than man, such general providence, they argued, would be enough.

While admitting that creatures such as animals do not have the particular providence which God has for men and angels, Thomas nevertheless insists that this is due to the nature of animals, not to any inability or limitation on the part of God to know animals or to provide for them. "God knows all particular beings perfectly . . . all individual things, even as individuals, fall under God's providence." Since God creates all beings, He knows all beings and keeps them in existence—even in their individual characteristics. Thus, through His all-embracing causality, God is able to exercise Providence over all reality.

In the case of man, St. Thomas notes, since he is through his freedom "the cause of his own action": he is able to provide for himself in a large measure. Yet every man has his final end established for him. It is at once the burden and the dignity of man that possession of this final end, the vision of God, involves freedom of choice. St. Thomas observes in this conjunction that if when providing for their future men choose in keeping with their dignity and destiny

God's providence arranges that "nothing will happen to them that is not for their own good, and everything that happens will be to their own advantage." This is the kind of providence that is proper to the human person. But if a man should want to live like an animal, he must accept the laws that apply to animals, whose individual good is inconsequential since they exist primarily for others. "If in their own providence men do not keep that order which is congruent with their dignity as rational creatures, but provide after the manner of brute animals, then God's providence will dispose of them according to the order that belongs to brutes, so that their good and evil acts will not be directed to their own profit but to the profit of others." If a man wishes to live like an animal, God will treat him as one. However impressive this stern view might be, it is not typical of St. Thomas, whose kindness and charity to all, even to the hardest of sinners, was remarked by his contemporaries.

When he discusses in this work the role played by celestial spheres in determining the sex of children and their disposition, St. Thomas follows Aristotle and the opinions of the day, granting the spheres a greater role than modern science would allow. Celestial spheres were thought to have the same influence on bodily chemistry as we currently ascribe to cosmic rays, so it must not be thought that these passages testify to even a passing weakness for astrology on the part of the Saint.

Having discussed the general question of God's providence and plan for His creatures, St. Thomas then takes up the infinitely more delicate problem of predestination. As a free agent, man is responsible for all acts which he undertakes after sufficient reflection. Yet the faith that arises from Jewish and Christian traditions clearly speaks of God's foreknowledge and predestination. How is this possible? If God knows what man is going to do, how can a man be free to act or not to act? And if a man is foreknown or predestined to Heaven, it would seem that whatever good he does or whatever evil he brings about is irrelevant to his final destiny. How does God know that a man will infallibly go to Hell or to Heaven? Is it because of some decree whereby God assigns someone to his final destiny? And if God knows that a man is predestined to Hell, why does He create him in the first place?

These are the same problems that terrified Kierkegaard and, for that matter, they are the problems that beset any serious Christian or Jew who believes in divine foreknowledge and predestination. Thomists themselves dispute over what was actually St. Thomas's final position on many of these questions. It should be noted, however, that St. Thomas approaches the basic problem in a manner that makes meaningless such questions as "If God knows that a man will be damned, why does He create him at all?" For throughout the entire sections on divine prov-

idence and predestination St. Thomas insists on
the timelessness of God's eternity. God exists in
an eternal now, standing outside of time, just
as He stands outside of space. Hence the proposition "If God knows a man will be damned,
he will be damned" should be converted into
the present tense and should read "If God knows
a man is damned, he is damned," for God sees
the damnation as actually taking place. Here, of
course, we are involved in the mystery where it
should be, i.e., in the divine nature, and are not
attempting to resolve absurdities and contradic-
tions.

St. Thomas creates a similar context for the
problems centering around man's free acts. If
God wills that an act take place freely, it will
take place freely because in His knowledge He
sees it taking place freely. What God wills will
take place, but when God produces a contingent
or free effect He does so, not through a necessitating but through a contingent cause. Otherwise freedom would be destroyed; and to St.
Thomas, as to Sartre, human freedom is so
obvious a part of immediate experience that it
cannot be contradicted without involving all experience in absurdity.

It is unlikely that St. Thomas himself ever
felt that he had fully resolved the infallibility of
predestination with our freedom of choice, but
it is evidently clear that as a Christian he re-
fused to accept one without the other. In the
present work (question 6, article 3), he ventures

a theory whereby God, as it were, is described
as wearing down the resistance of one predestined
by flooding him with graces to such a point that
he can no longer refuse the divine generosity and
tiredly but freely accepts salvation. That this
was freedom of a feeble sort St. Thomas himself
seems to have realized, for the theory does not
recur in any of his later works.

To most men the problem of predestination
is intimately connected with the problem of sin.
Throughout *Truth* as well as his other writings,
St. Thomas speaks of sin as being falsity and
non-being, i.e., an absurd absence of a goodness
which should be **pres**ent but is not. Sin is something irrational, a surd that cannot be reduced
to intelligible factors. It excludes understanding,
for when a man chooses to depart from the
order which has been divinely established for
him, he is trying to be something other than
what he actually is. It is this attempt that renders
his existence schizoid and agonizing. At the mo-
ment of death, when further choice is no longer
possible, the will of the sinner remains fixed
upon the finite good which he had prized above
all—even above God, and this perversion of the
will remains forever. "The souls of the damned
will inhere forever in the end which they have
chosen." That which they have prized above all
and chosen as their greatest good will be finally
given to them for all eternity—but nothing else.
(*Summa Contra Gentes*, IV, c. 93). This theory
described by Thomas is dramatically **portrayed**

by Dante in the *Inferno* where he describes one of the lowest depths of Hell as a glacial region where the damned have their jaws locked in the necks of those whom they hate. In life they loved their hatred more than they loved God; in death they have their hatred but nothing more.

In this view, then, sin is something depraved and irrational. Consequently, it cannot be explained or reduced to any divine plan or purpose. It is permitted by God, and St. Thomas seems to feel that it could be excluded by Him only through the destruction of human freedom. As the absence of goodness that should be present, sin has no existence or being of its own. It is understood only through its relationship to its opposite, somewhat as blindness is understood as being the absence of sight. St. Thomas never held, like some of his contemporaries, that matter was evil. He was one of the strongest opponents of the Albigensian heretics who held that the body was sinful and that marriage was unholy. For him the mystery of iniquity was partly that sin should arise at all in a universe in which all that is, is good.

As we have seen, then, St. Thomas insists that the entire problem of predestination be viewed in the context of God's eternal presentness. It is only in the metaphysics of God as living in an everlasting now that any meaningful understanding of the infallibility of His knowledge and the irresistibility of His will can ever be achieved.

The mystery still remains, of course. But these sections of *Truth* constitute some of St. Thomas's finest efforts to speculate from the data of Christian faith. They are his response to the challenge of Christianity as a "fides quaerens intellectum" —as a faith seeking understanding, a faith beckoning to the intellect to participate of its riches. Although St. Thomas was convinced that the intellect can never exhaust the instrinsic intelligibility of Christian revelation, he felt that any knowledge of God, however imperfect, was preferable to the perfect knowledge of anything else.

Robert W. Mulligan, S.J., Ph.D.
Loyola University, Chicago

Providence

ARTICLE I

This Question Treats Providence. In the First Article We Ask: To WHICH ATTRIBUTE CAN GOD'S PROVIDENCE BE REDUCED?

Difficulties:

It seems that it belongs only to His knowledge, for

1. Boethius says: "It is certainly clear that Providence is the immovable and simple form of things to be done." Now, in God the form of things that should be done is an idea, and an idea pertains to His knowledge. Providence, therefore, pertains to His knowledge.

2. But it was said that providence also pertains to God's will in so far as it is the cause of things. To the contrary, in us practical knowledge causes the things that we know. Practical knowledge, however, consists merely in knowledge. The same is true, therefore, of providence.

3. In the same section as cited above, Boethius writes: "The plan of carrying things out, when considered in the purity of God's understanding, is called Providence." Now, purity of understand-

ing seems to pertain to speculative knowledge. Providence, therefore, pertains to speculative knowledge.

4. Boethius writes: "Providence is so called because, standing at a distance from the lowest things, it looks upon all things from their highest summit." Now, to look upon is to know, especially to know speculatively. Providence, therefore, seems to belong to speculative knowledge.

5. As Boethius says: "Fate is related to Providence as reasoning is to understanding." Now, understanding and reasoning are common to both speculative and practical knowledge. Providence, therefore, also belongs to both types of knowledge.

6. Augustine writes: "An unchangeable law controls all changeable things, governing them gloriously." Now, control and government belong to providence. Consequently, that unchangeable law is providence itself. But law pertains to knowledge. Therefore, providence also belongs to knowledge.

7. The natural law as it exists within us is caused by divine providence. Now, a cause acts to bring about an effect in its own likeness. For this reason we also say that God's goodness is the cause of goodness in things, His essence, the cause of their being, and His life, the cause of their living. Divine providence, therefore, is a law; hence, our former position stands.

8. Boethius says: "Providence is the divine plan set up within the ruler of all things." Now,

as Augustine says, the divine plan of a thing is an idea. Providence, therefore, is an idea; and since an idea pertains to knowledge, providence also pertains to knowledge.

9. Practical knowledge is ordained either to bring things into existence or to order things already in existence. Now, it does not belong to providence to bring things into existence. It rather presupposes the things over which it is exercised. Nor does it order things that are in existence. This belongs to God's disposal of things. Providence, therefore, pertains not to practical, but only to speculative knowledge.

To the Contrary:

1'. Providence seems to belong to the will, because, as Damascene says: "Providence is the will of God, which brings all existing things to a suitable end."

2'. We do not call those people provident who know what to do but are unwilling to do it. Providence, therefore, is related more to the will than to knowledge.

3'. As Boethius says, God governs the world by His goodness. Now, goodness pertains to the will. Therefore, providence also pertains to the will, since the role of providence is to govern.

4'. To dispose things is a function, not of knowledge, but of will. Now, according to Boethius, providence is the plan according to which God disposes all things. Providence, therefore, pertains to the will, not to knowledge.

5'. What is provided for, taken simply as such, is neither a wise thing nor a known thing. It is merely a good. Consequently, one who provides, taken as such, is not wise, but good. Hence, providence does not pertain to wisdom, but to goodness or to the will.

To the Contrary (Second Series):

1'. Furthermore, it seems that providence pertains to power. For Boethius says: "Providence has given to the things it has created the greatest reason for enduring, so that as far as they are able, all things naturally desire to endure." Providence, therefore, is a principle of creation. But, since creation is appropriated to God's power, providence pertains to power.

2'. Government is the effect of providence, for the Book of Wisdom (14:3) says: "But thy providence, O Father, governeth all." But, as Hugh of St. Victor says, the will commands, wisdom directs, and power executes. Power, therefore, is more closely related to government than is knowledge or will. Consequently, providence pertains more to power than to knowledge or will.

REPLY:

Because our intellects are weak, what we know of God we have to learn from creatures around us. Consequently, to know how God is said to be provident, we have to see how creatures are provident.

We should first note that Cicero makes providence a part of prudence. Providence, as it were, completes prudence, since the other two parts of prudence, memory and understanding, are merely preparations for the prudent act. Moreover, according to the Philosopher, prudence is the reasoned plan of doing things. Now, things to be done differ from things to be made, because the latter start from an agent and terminate in some extrinsic matter, as, for example, a bench and a house; and the reasoned plan of making them is called art. On the other hand, things to be done are actions which do not go outside the agent, but, instead, are acts that perfect him, as, for example, chaste living, bearing oneself patiently, and the like. The reasoned plan of performing these is called prudence. With respect to action, two things should be considered: the end and the means.

However, it is especially the role of prudence to direct the means to the end; and, as we read in the *Ethics,* one is called prudent if he deliberates well. But, as we also read in the *Ethics,* deliberation "is not concerned with ends, but only with means." Now, the end of things to be done pre-exists in us in two ways: first, through the natural knowledge we have of man's end. This knowledge, of course, as the Philosopher says, belongs to the intellect, which is a principle of things to be done as well as of things to be studied; and, as the Philosopher also points out, ends are principles of things to be done. The second way that these ends pre-exist in us is through our desires. Here the ends of things to be done exist in us in our moral virtues, which influence a man to live a just, brave, or temperate life. This is in a sense, the proximate end of things to be done. We are similarly perfected with respect to the means toward this end: our knowledge is perfected by counsel, our appetite, by choice; and in these matters we are directed by prudence.

It is clear, therefore, that it belongs to prudence to dispose, in any orderly way, the means towards an end. And because this disposing of means to an end is done by prudence, it can be said to take place by a kind of reasoning process, whose first principles are ends. The very reason for the sequence described above—and found in all things to be done—is taken from ends, as is clear in the case of art products. Consequently, if one would be prudent, he must stand in the proper relation to the ends themselves, for a reasoned plan cannot exist unless the principles of reason are maintained. Hence, prudence requires not only the understanding of ends but also moral virtues by which the will is settled in a correct end. For this reason, the Philosopher says that the prudent man must be virtuous. Finally, this is common to all rightly ordered powers and acts of the soul: the virtue of what is first is maintained in all the rest. Consequently, in prudence, in some way, are included both the will as directed toward an end and the knowledge of the end itself.

From what has been said it is now clear how providence is related to God's other attributes. His knowledge is related both to ends and to means toward ends, because through knowledge God knows Himself and creatures. But providence pertains only to that knowledge which is concerned with means to ends and in so far as these means are ordained to ends. Consequently, in God providence includes both knowledge and will, although, taken essentially, it belongs only to knowledge, that is, to practical, not to speculative, knowledge. Providence, moreover, also includes the power of execution; hence, an act of power presupposes an act of providence, as it were, directing it, and for this reason power is not included in providence as the will is.

Answers to Difficulties:

1. Two aspects of a creature can be considered: first, its species taken absolutely; second, its relation to an end. The form of each exists previously in God. The exemplary form of a thing considered absolutely in its species is an idea; but the form of a thing considered as directed to an end is called providence. Moreover, according to Boethius, the order divine providence implants in things is called fate. Consequently, providence is related to fate as an idea is related to the species of a thing. An idea, however, can in some way pertain to speculative knowledge; but providence is related only to practical knowledge, since it implies an ordering to an end, and,

consequently, to something to be done, by means of which the end will be reached.

2. Providence pertains more to the will than does practical knowledge taken absolutely, because the latter is concerned in general only with the knowledge of an end and of the means to achieve it. Consequently, practical knowledge does not presuppose that an end has been willed. If this were true, then the will would be included in knowledge, as has been said with regard to providence.

3. Purity of understanding is mentioned, not to exclude the will from the concept of providence, but to exclude change and mutability.

4. In this passage Boethius is not giving a complete description of the nature of providence. He is merely giving the reason for its name. Consequently, even though looking upon things may be considered a speculative knowledge, it does not follow that providence may be considered to be such. Besides, Boethius explains providence, or foresight, as though it were farsight, because "God Himself surveys all things from their highest summit." But God is on the highest summit of things for the very reason that He causes and directs all things. So, even in the words of Boethius something pertaining to practical knowledge can be noted.

5. The comparison Boethius makes is taken from the resemblance had by the proportion between the simple and the composite to the proportion between a body at rest and a body in

motion. For, just as understanding is simple and non-discursive but reason is discursive, passing from one thing to another, similarly, providence is simple and unchangeable but fate is multiple and changeable. The conclusion, therefore, does not follow.

6. Properly speaking, God's providence is not the eternal law; it is something that follows upon the eternal law. The eternal law should be thought of as existing in God as those principles of action exist in us which we know naturally and upon which we base our deliberation and choice. These belong to prudence or providence. Consequently, the law of our intellect is related to prudence as an indemonstrable principle is related to a demonstration. Similarly, the eternal law in God is not His providence, but, as it were, a principle of His providence; for this reason one can, without any inconsistency, attribute an act of providence to the eternal law in the same way that he attributes every conclusion of a demonstration to self-evident principles.

7. There are two types of causality to be found in the divine attributes. The first type is exemplary causality. Because of this type, we say that all living beings come from the first living being. This type of causality is common to all the divine attributes. The second type of causality is according to the relation the attributes have to their objects. We say, for example, that divine power is the cause of the possibles, divine knowledge is the cause of what is known. An effect of

this type of causality need not resemble its cause; for the things that are made by knowledge need not be knowledge, but merely known. It is according to this type of causality that the providence of God is said to be the cause of all things. Consequently, even though the natural law within our understanding is derived from providence, it does not follow that divine providence is the eternal law.

8. "That divine plan within the highest ruler" is not called providence unless one includes in it the notion of direction to an end, which, in turn, presupposes that an end has been willed. Consequently, even though providence may essentially belong to knowledge, it also, in some way, includes the divine will.

9. A twofold ordering may be found in things. First, there is that order according to which things come from their principles. Second, there is the order according to which they are directed to an end. Now, the divine disposing pertains to that order according to which things proceed from their principles; for things are said to be disposed inasmuch as they are put on different levels by God, who is like an artist arranging the different parts of his work in different ways. Consequently, disposition seems to pertain to art. Providence, however, implies the ordering which directs to an end; for this reason it differs from the divine art and disposition. For divine art is so called because of its relation to the production

of things, but divine disposition is so called because of its relation to the order of what has already been produced. Providence, however, implies the ordination to an end. Now, we can gather from the end of an art product whatever exists in the thing itself. Moreover, the ordering of a thing to an end is more closely related to the end than is the ordering of its parts to each other. In fact, their ordering to an end is, in a sense, the cause of the ordering of the parts to each other. Consequently, divine providence is, in a sense, the cause of God's disposition of things, and for this reason an act of His disposition is sometimes attributed to His providence. Therefore, even if providence is not an art related to the production of things or a disposition related to the ordering of things one to another, it does not follow that providence does not belong to practical knowledge.

Answers to Contrary Difficulties:

1'. With reference to the difficulty about the will, we reply that Damascene calls providence will inasmuch as providence includes and presupposes the will, as we have pointed out previously.

2'. As the Philosopher says, no man can be prudent unless he has moral virtues which rightly dispose him toward his ends, just as no one can demonstrate properly unless he knows well the principles of demonstration. It is for this reason that no one is said to be provident unless he has a correct will—not because providence is in the will.

3'. God is said to govern through His goodness, not because His goodness is providence, but because, having the nature of an end, His goodness is a principle of providence. He is also said to govern through His goodness because the divine goodness is related to God as moral virtues are to us.

4'. Even though the disposition of things presupposes the will, it is not an act of the will, because, as the Philosopher says, ordering, which is what is meant by disposition, is the act of one who is wise. Consequently, both disposition and providence really belong to knowledge.

5'. Providence is compared to what is provided for as knowledge is compared to what is known—not as knowledge is compared to the knower. Consequently, it is not necessary that what is foreseen, taken as such, be wise, but rather that it be known.

The other two arguments we concede.

ARTICLE II

In the Second Article We Ask: Is THE WORLD
RULED BY PROVIDENCE?

Difficulties:

It seems that it is not, for

1. No agent that acts from natural necessity
acts through providence. But God acts upon
created things through the necessity of nature,
because, as Dionysius says: "The divine goodness
communicates itself to us like the sun, which,
without previous choice or knowledge, pours out
its rays upon all bodies." The world, therefore,
is not ruled by the providence of God.

2. A principle having many forms is posterior
to a principle having but one form. Now, the will
is a multiform principle because it is related to
opposites. Consequently, providence is also multiform, since it presupposes will. On the other
hand, nature is a principle having but one form,
because it is determined to one. Therefore,
nature precedes providence. Consequently, the
realm of nature is not ruled by providence.

3. But it was said that a principle having one
form precedes a multiform principle in the same
genus, not in other genera.—On the contrary,
the greater the power that a principle has of
exercising causality, the greater is its priority.

But the more a principle has but one form, the greater is its power of causality, since, as said in *The Causes:* "A united power is more infinite than one that is multiplied." Consequently, a principle having but one form precedes a multiform principle whether they are in the same genus or in different genera.

4. According to Boethius, any inequality is reduced to an equality and any multitude to a unity. Therefore, any multiple act of the will ought to be reduced to an act of nature that is simple and equal. Hence, the first cause must work through its own essence and nature, and not through providence. Thus, our original argument stands.

5. What is, of itself, determined to one course of action does not need the direction of anything else, because direction is applied to a thing to prevent it from taking a contrary course. Natural things, however, are determined to one course of action by their own natures. Consequently, they do not need the direction of providence.

6. But it was said that natural things need the direction of providence to be kept in being.—On the contrary, if no possibility of corruption exists in a thing, it has no need of something extrinsic to conserve it. Now, there are some things in which there is no potency to corruption, since there is none to generation, as, for example, the celestial bodies and the spiritual substances, which are the most important things in the uni-

verse. Therefore, substances of this sort do not need providence to keep them in being.

7. There are certain things in the realm of nature that even God cannot change, such as the principle that "one cannot assert and deny the same thing under the same aspect," and "what has existed cannot not have existed," as Augustine says. Therefore, at least principles of this sort do not need divine rule and conservation.

8. Damascene points out that it would be illogical to say that the one who makes things is other than the one who exercises providence over them. Material bodies, however, are not made by God, since He is a spirit, and it seems no more possible for a spirit to produce a material body than for a material body to produce a spirit. Material bodies of this sort, therefore, are not ruled through divine providence.

9. The government of things involves distinguishing between things. But making things distinct does not seem to be the work of God, because, as said in *The Causes,* God is related to all things in one way. Therefore, things are not ruled through divine providence.

10. Things ordered of themselves need not be ordered by others. But natural things are ordered of themselves, because, as is said in *The Soul:* "For all things naturally constituted there is a term and proportion set to their size and growth." Natural things, therefore, are not ordered by divine providence.

11. If things were ruled by divine providence, we could know divine providence by studying the order of nature. But, as Damascene says: "We should wonder at all things, praise all things, and accept without question all the works of providence." The world, therefore, is not ruled by providence.

To the Contrary:

1'. Boethius writes: "O Thou that dost the world in everlasting order guide!"

2'. Whatever has a fixed order must be ruled by a providence. But natural things have a fixed order in their motions. Hence, they are ruled by providence.

3'. Things which have different natures remain joined only if they are ruled by a providence. For this reason, certain philosophers were forced to say that the soul is a harmony, because contraries remain joined together in the bodies of animals. Now, we see that in the world contraries and things of different natures are kept together. Consequently, the world is ruled by providence.

4'. As Boethius says: "Fate directs the motion of all things and determines their places, forms, and time. This unfolding of the temporal order, united in the foresight of God's mind, is providence." Therefore, since we see that things have distinct forms, times, or places, we must admit the existence of fate and, consequently, that of providence.

5′. Whatever cannot keep itself in existence needs something else to rule it and keep it in existence. But created things cannot keep themselves in existence, for, as Damascene says, what is made from nothing tends, of itself, to return to nothing. There must, therefore, be a providence ruling over things.

REPLY:

Providence is concerned with the direction of things to an end. Therefore, as the Commentator says, whoever denies final causality should also deny providence. Now, those who deny final casuality take two positions.

Some of the very ancient philosophers admitted only a material cause. Since they would not admit an efficient cause, they could not affirm the existence of an end, for an end is a cause only in so far as it moves the efficient cause. Other and later philosophers admitted an efficient cause, but said nothing about a final cause. According to both schools, everything was necessarily caused by previously existing causes, material or efficient.

This position, however, was criticized by other philosophers on the following grounds. Material and efficient causes, as such, cause only the existence of their effects. They are not sufficient to produce goodness in them so that they be aptly disposed in themselves, so that they could continue to exist, and toward others so that they could help them. Heat, for example, of its very nature and of itself can break down other things, but this breaking down is good and helpful only if it happens up to a certain point and in a certain way. Consequently, if we do not admit that there exist in nature causes other than heat and similar agents, we cannot give any reason why things happen in a good and orderly way.

Moreover, whatever does not have a determinate cause happens by accident. Consequently, if the position mentioned above were true, all the harmony and usefulness found in things would be the result of chance. This was actually what Empedocles held. He asserted that it was by accident that the parts of animals came together in this way through friendship—and this was his explanation of an animal and of a frequent occurrence! This explanation, of course, is absurd, for those things that happen by chance, happen only rarely; we know from experience, however, that harmony and usefulness are found in nature either at all times or at least for the most part. This cannot be the result of mere chance; it must be because an end is intended. What lacks intellect or knowledge, however, cannot tend directly toward an end. It can do this only if someone else's knowledge has established an end for it, and directs it to that end. Consequently, since natural things have no knowledge, there must be some previously existing intelligence directing them to an end, like an archer who gives a definite motion to an arrow so that it will wing its way to a determined end. Now, the hit made by the arrow is said to be the work not of the arrow alone but also of the person who shot it. Similarly, philosophers call every work of nature the work of intelligence.

Consequently, the world is ruled by the providence of that intellect which gave this order to nature; and we may compare the providence by which God rules the world to the domestic foresight by which a man rules his family, or to the political foresight by which a ruler governs a city or a kingdom, and directs the acts of others to a definite end. There is no providence, however, in God with respect to Himself, since whatever is in Him is an end, not a means to it.

Answers to Difficulties:

1. The metaphor used by Dionysius notes merely that, like the sun which, on its own part, keeps no body from sharing its light, the divine goodness keeps no creature from participating in itself. The metaphor does not mean that providence acts without choice or knowledge.

2. A principle can be said to be multiform in two senses. First, the multiformity can refer to the very essence of the principle—that is, the principle is composite. A principle that is multiform in this sense must be posterior to a principle having but one form. Second, the multiformity may refer to the principle's relation to its effects, so that a principle is said to be multiform because it extends its influence to many things. A principle that is multiform in this sense precedes

one that has but a single form, because the more simple a principle is, the more extensive is its influence. It is in this sense, moreover, that the will is said to be a multiform, and nature, a uniform principle.

3. The argument given is based on the uniformity of a principle according to its essence.

4. God is the cause of things by His essence. Consequently, any plurality in things can be reduced to one simple principle. His essence, however, is the cause of things only in so far as it is known, and consequently, only in so far as it wills to be communicated to a creature by the creature's being made in its likeness. Hence, things proceed from the divine essence through the ordering of knowledge and will, and so through providence.

5. That determination by which a natural thing is restricted to one course of action belongs to it, not because of itself, but because of something else. Consequently, the very determination for bringing about the suitable effect is, as has been said, a proof of divine providence.

6. Generation and corruption can be understood in two senses. First, generation and corruption can arise from a contrary being and terminate in a contrary. In this sense, the potency to generation and corruption exists in a thing because its matter is in potency to contrary forms; and in this respect celestial bodies and spiritual substances have no potency to generation or corruption. Second, these terms are commonly used

to indicate any coming into or passing out of existence that is found in things. Consequently, even creation, by which a thing is drawn from nothingness into existence, is called generation; and the annihilation of a thing is called corruption.

Moreover, a thing is said to be in potency to generation in this sense if an agent has the power to produce it; and it is said to be in potency to corruption if an agent has the power to reduce it to nothingness. In this way of speaking, every creature is in potency to corruption; for all that God has brought into existence He can also reduce to nothingness. For, as Augustine says, for creatures to subsist God must constantly work in them. This action of God, however, must not be compared to the action of a craftsman building a house, for, when his action ceases, the house still remains; it should rather be compared to the sun's lighting up the air. Consequently, when God no longer gives existence to a creature, whose very existence depends on His will, then this creature is reduced to nothingness.

7. The necessity of the principles mentioned depends upon God's providence and disposition, because the fact that created things have a particular nature and, in this nature, a determined act of existence, makes these things distinct from their negations; and upon this distinction is based the principle that affirmation and negation cannot be true simultaneously. Moreover, on this principle, as we read in the *Metaphysics,* the

necessity of all the other principles is founded.

8. An effect cannot be stronger than its cause. It can, however, be weaker than its cause. Now, since body is naturally inferior to spirit, it cannot produce a spirit; but a spirit can produce a body.

9. God is similarly said to be related to all things, because there is no diversity in Him. He is, however, the cause of diversity in things inasmuch as by His knowledge He contains within Himself the intelligible characters of all things.

10. That order which is found in nature is not caused by nature but by something else. Consequently, nature needs providence to implant such an order in it.

11. Creatures fail to represent their creator adequately. Consequently, through them we cannot arrive at a perfect knowledge of God. Another reason for our imperfect knowledge is the weakness of our intellect, which cannot assimilate all the evidence of God that is to be found in creatures. It is for this reason that we are forbidden to scrutinize God's attributes overzealously in the sense of aiming at the completion of such an inquiry, an aim which is implied in the very notion of overzealous scrutiny. If we were to act thus, we would not believe anything about God unless our intellect could grasp it. We are not, however, kept from humbly investigating God's attributes, remembering that we are too weak to arrive at a perfect comprehension of Him. Consequently, Hilary writes as follows:

"Even if a man who reverently seeks the infinite ways of God never reaches the end of his search, his search will always profit him."

ARTICLE III

In the Third Article We Ask: DOES GOD'S PROVIDENCE EXTEND TO CORRUPTIBLE THINGS?

Difficulties:

It seems that it does not, for

1. A cause and its effects are in the same order. Now, corruptible creatures are the cause of sin. This is evident. For example, women's beauty is an incitement to and cause of lust. Moreover, Wisdom (14:11) says: "The creatures of God have been turned into . . . a snare for the feet of the unwise." Now, since sin is outside the order of divine providence, it seems that corruptible beings are not subject to this order.

2. Nothing that a wise man arranges can destroy his work, because he would be contradicting himself were he to build and destroy the same thing. Now, we find among corruptible things some that are contrary to and destructive of others. Consequently, corruptible things were not arranged by God.

3. Damascene speaks as follows: "It must be true that all things happening according to God's

providence take place according to right reason in a way that is best and most fitting in God's eyes—indeed, in a way that is better for them to take place." But corruptible things could become better, for they could become incorruptible. The providence of God, therefore, does not extend to corruptible things.

4. Whatever is corruptible has corruption in it by its very nature; otherwise it would not be necessary for all corruptible things to corrupt. But, since corruption is a defect, it is not provided for by God, who cannot be a cause of any defect. Corruptible natures, therefore, do not come under God's providence.

5. As Dionysius says, providence does not destroy nature but saves it. The role of God's providence, therefore, is to save things continually. But corruptible things are not continually saved. They are not, therefore, subject to God's providence.

To the Contrary:

1'. Wisdom (14:3) says: "But thy Providence, O Father, governeth all things."

2'. Wisdom (12:13) also says that it is God who "hast care of all things." Therefore, corruptible as well as incorruptible things fall under His providence.

3'. As Damascene says, it is illogical to hold that one being creates things and another exercises providence over them. Now, God is the efficient cause of all corruptible things. Consequently, He also provides for them.

REPLY:

As we said above, the providence by which God rules things is similar to the providence by which the father of a family rules his household or a king rules a city or kingdom. The common element in these rules is the primacy of the common good over the good of the individual; for, as we read in the *Ethics,* the good of the nation is more divine than that of the city, family, or person. Consequently, whoever is supervising must —if he is to rule wisely—pay more attention to what is good for the community than to what is good merely for an individual.

Some have not kept this point in mind, but considering only that there are corruptible things which, if taken in themselves, could be better, and not considering the order of the universe in which each and every thing is excellently arranged—some, I say, have said that those corruptible things are therefore not ruled by God but that only incorruptible things are. These persons are represented in Job (22:14) by the man who says: "The clouds are God's covert, and he doth not consider our things, and he walketh about the poles of heaven." Moreover, they assert that corruptible things act necessarily and without any ruler at all or are ruled by an opposing principle. The Philosopher, however, has refuted this position by taking an army as an example. In an army we find two orders, one by which the parts of the army are related to each other, and a second by which the army is directed to an external good, namely, the good of its leader. That order by which the parts of the army are related to each other exists for the sake of the order by which the entire army is subordinated to its leader. Consequently, if the subordination to the leader did not exist, the ordering of the parts of the army to each other would not exist. Consequently, whenever we find a group whose members are ordered to each other, that group must necessarily be ordered to some external principle.

Now, the corruptible and incorruptible parts of the universe are related to each other essentially, not accidentally. For we see that corruptible bodies benefit from celestial bodies, and always, or at least ordinarily, in the same manner. Consequently, all things, corruptible and incorruptible, must be in one order under the providence of an external principle outside the universe. For this reason, the Philosopher concluded that it was necessary to affirm the existence of a single rule over the universe, and of not more than one.

It must be noted, however, that a thing is provided for in two ways: for itself, or for other things. For example, in a home, care is taken of some things on their own account, namely, those things that constitute the essential goods of a household, such as sons, possessions, and the like; and other things, such as utensils, animals, and the like are cared for so that the essential things can use them. Similarly, in the universe, the things in which the essential perfection of the universe consists are provided for on their own account, and like the universe itself, these things stay in existence. But the things that do not endure are provided for, not for their own sake, but for the sake of other things. Consequently, spiritual substances and heavenly bodies, which are perpetual both as species and as individuals, are provided for on their own account both as species and as individuals. Corruptible things, however, are perpetual only as a species; hence, these species are looked after for their own sake, but the individual members of these species are not provided for except for this reason: to keep the species in perpetual existence.

If we thus understand the opinion of those who say that divine providence does not extend to corruptible things of this kind, except as they participate in the nature of a species, it need not be rejected; for this opinion is true if it is understood as referring to the providence of things by which they are provided for on their own account.

Answers to Difficulties:

1. Of themselves, corruptible creatures do not cause sin. They are only its occasion and accidental cause. Now, an accidental cause and its

effect do not have to belong to the same order.

2. A wise provider does not consider what is good for merely one of the things that fall under his providence. He is concerned rather with what is better for all. Consequently, even though the corruption of a thing in the universe is not good for that thing, it is good for the perfection of the entire universe, because the continual generation and corruption of individuals makes it possible for the species to be perpetual; and it is in this that the perfection of the universe essentially consists.

3. Although a corruptible thing would be better if it possessed incorruptibility, it is better for the universe to be made of both corruptible and incorruptible things than to be merely of the latter, because the nature of the corruptible thing, as well as that of the incorruptible, is good, and it is better to have two goods than merely one. Moreover, multiplication of individuals in one nature is of less value than a variety of natures, since the good found in a nature, being communicable, is superior to the good found in an individual, which is incommunicable.

4. Darkness is brought about by the sun, not because of any action of the sun, but because the sun does not send out light. Similarly, corruption comes from God, not because of any positive action by Him, but because He does not give the thing permanency.

5. The things that are provided for by **God**

on their own account last forever. But this permanency is not necessary for those things that are not provided for on their own account. These need remain only so long as they are needed by the things for which they are provided. Consequently, as is clear from the previous discussion, certain things corrupt because they are not looked after for their own sakes.

ARTICLE IV

In the Fourth Article We Ask: ARE THE MOTIONS AND ACTIONS OF ALL BODIES HERE BELOW SUBJECT TO DIVINE PROVIDENCE?

Difficulties:

It seems that they are not, for

1. God does not provide for a thing if He is not its author, because, as Damascene says, it is illogical to say that one person makes a thing and another provides for it. Now, God is not the author of evil, for to the extent that things come from Him they are good. Therefore, since many evil things happen in the actions and motions of creatures here below, it does not seem that all of their motions fall under His divine providence.

2. Motions that are contrary do not seem to belong to the same order. Now, in creatures here below there are contrary motions and actions.

Consequently, it is impossible that they all fall under the order of divine providence.

3. A thing falls under divine providence only inasmuch as it is directed to an end. But evil is not ordered to an end. On the contrary, it is a privation of order. Consequently, evil does not fall under providence. In creatures here below, however, many evils occur. Therefore:

4. A man is not prudent if he allows something evil to occur in those things whose actions fall under his providence when he can prevent that evil from taking place. Now, God is most prudent and powerful. Hence, since many evils occur in creatures here below, it seems that certain of their acts do not fall under divine providence.

5. It was said, however, that God permits these evils to happen because He can draw good from them. On the contrary, good is more powerful than evil, so it is easier to draw good from good than good from evil. Consequently, it is not necessary for God to permit evil to happen in order to draw good from it.

6. As Boethius says, just as God creates all things through His goodness so does He also govern all things by His goodness. But His divine goodness does not permit Him to make anything evil. Consequently, His goodness does not permit anything evil to come under His providence.

7. If a thing is arranged, it does not happen by chance. Therefore, if all the motions of creatures here below were arranged, nothing

would happen by chance, but everything would happen by necessity. This, however, is impossible.

8. As the Commentator says, if everything happened in creatures here below because of the necessity of matter, they would not be ruled by providence. But many things in creatures here below happen because of the necessity of matter. At least these events, then, are not ruled by providence.

9. No prudent man permits a good so that evil will result. For the same reason, therefore, no prudent man permits an evil that good will result. Since God is prudent, He will therefore not permit evils in order that good will result. Consequently, it seems that the evils occurring in creatures here below are not allowed by providence.

10. What is blameworthy in a man should by no means be attributed to God. But a man is blamed if he does wrong in order to get something good. This is clear from the Epistle to the Romans (3:8): "As we are slandered, and as some affirm that we say: 'Let us do evil, that there may come good.'" Consequently, it is contrary to God's nature for evil to come under His providence in order that good may be drawn from it.

11. If the acts of bodies here below were subject to God's providence, they would act in harmony with God's justice. But the lower elements do not act in this way: fire burns the

homes of the just as well as those of the unjust. Consequently, acts of lower bodies do not fall under God's providence.

To the Contrary:

1'. In the Gospel according to Matthew (10:29), we read: "Are not two sparrows sold for a farthing? and not one of them shall fall on the ground without your Father." On this, the *Gloss* reads: "Great is the providence of God. Not even the smallest things escape it." Consequently, even the smallest movement of things here below comes under God's providence.

2'. Augustine writes as follows: "It is because of God's providence that we see celestial bodies ordered from on high, stars and planets of the earth shining down on us below, the regular alternation of night and day, the rugged earth being cleansed by surrounding waves of water, air gushing out in the heavens, shrubs and animals being conceived and born, growing, wasting away, and killing, and all things else that happen by interior, natural motion." Consequently, all motions of lower bodies fall under God's providence.

REPLY:

Since the first principle of things is the same as their final end, things come from their first principle and are ordered to their ultimate end in the same manner. Studying things as they come from their principle, however, we find that those which are close to their principle have an unfailing act of existence, but, as is said in *Generation and Corruption,* those that are remote from their principle have a corruptible act of existence. Consequently, with respect to their relation to an end, those things that are closest to their ultimate end unfailingly keep their direction to their end, but those that are remote from their ultimate end sometimes diverge from their direction to it.

Moreover, the same things that are close to their principle are close to their end, and those that are remote from their principle are remote from their end. Consequently, not only have incorruptible substances an unfailing act of existence, but also their actions never fail to keep their direction to an end. For example, there are heavenly bodies whose motions never leave their natural orbit. However, because corruptible bodies have defective natures, many of their movements diverge from their proper order. It is for this reason that, in regard to the order of the universe, the Philosopher compares incorruptible bodies to children in a household who always do what is good for the home, and corruptible bodies to domestic animals and slaves whose actions frequently violate the order laid down by the one in charge of the household. This is the reason, too, why Avicenna says that nothing evil lies beyond the moon and that there is evil only in creatures here below.

It should not be thought, however, that those

acts of things here below which are outside their proper course are entirely outside the order of providence. For a thing comes under God's providence in two ways: it can be something to which something else is ordered or it can be something that is ordered to something else. Now, as said in the *Physics* and in the *Metaphysics,* in an order of means to an end, all the intermediate members are ends as well as means to an end. Consequently, whatever is rightly ordered by providence comes under providence not only as something that is referred to something else, but also as something to which another thing is referred. However, a thing which leaves the right order comes under providence only as something referred, to something else, not as something to which another thing has been referred. For example, the act of the generative powers by which one man generates another complete in his nature is directed by God to a particular thing, namely, a human form; and to the act itself something else is directed, namely, the generative power. A defective act which results occasionally in the generation of natural monstrosities is, of course, directed by God to some useful purpose; but to this defective act itself nothing else was directed. It happened merely on account of the failure of some cause. With regard to the first-named act of generation, the providence is one of approval; with regard to the second, it is one of permission. These two kinds of providence are discussed by Damascene.

It should be noted, however, that some have restricted God's providence to only the species of natural things, and have excluded it from individuals except as they participate in a common nature. They did this because they did not admit that God knows singulars, but said that God directs the nature of a species in such a way that the resultant power of a species can bring about a certain action, and, if this should fail at times, the failure itself is directed to something useful—just as the corruption of one thing is directed to the generation of another. They denied, however, that a particular force is directed to a particular act and that this particular failure is directed to this particular use. But since we say that God knows all particular things perfectly, we assert that all individual things, even as individuals, fall under God's providence.

Answers to Difficulties:

1. That argument touches only the providence of approval. It is true, however, that God does not provide for a thing unless He is in some way its author. Consequently, since evil does not come from God, it does not fall under His providence of approval, but falls only under His providence of permission.

2. Although contrary motions do not belong to

the same specific order, they do belong to one general order, as do even the different orders of different crafts which are subordinated to the order of a city.

3. Even though evil inasmuch as it issues from its own cause is without order and, for this reason, is defined as a privation of order, there is nothing that keeps a higher cause from ordering it. In this way evil comes under providence.

4. Any prudent man will endure a small evil in order that a great good will not be prevented. Any particular good, moreover, is trifling in comparison with the good of a universal nature. Again, evil cannot be kept from certain things without taking away their nature, which is such that it may or may not fail; and, while this nature may harm something in particular, it nevertheless gives some added beauty to the universe. Consequently, since God is most prudent, His providence does not prevent evil, but allows each thing to act as its nature requires it to act. For, as Dionysius says, the role of providence is to save, not to destroy, nature.

5. There are certain goods which can be drawn only from certain evils; for example, the good of patience can be drawn only from the evil of persecution, and the good of penitence only from the evil of sin. This, however, is not to deny that evil is weak in comparison with good, because things of this sort are drawn out of evil, not as from an essential cause, but, as it were, accidentally and materially.

6. Inasmuch as it has an act of existence, what ever is made must have the form of the one who makes it, because the making of a thing terminates in its act of existence. Consequently, an evil cannot be produced by a cause that is good. Now, providence directs a thing to an end, and this direction to an end follows upon the act of existence of the thing. It is not impossible, therefore, for something evil to be directed to a good by one who is good, but it is impossible for one who is good to direct something to an evil. For, just as the goodness of a maker puts the form of goodness in the things he makes, so also does the goodness of one who is provident put a direction to good in the things that are subject to his providence.

7. Effects happening accidentally in creatures here below can be considered in two ways: in their relation to proximate causes—and, in this sense, many things happen by chance—or in their relation to the first cause—and, in this sense, nothing in the world happens by chance. It does not follow, therefore, that all things happen necessarily, because in necessity and contingency effects do not follow first causes but proximate causes.

8. Those things resulting from the necessity of matter are themselves determined by natures ordered to an end, and for this reason can also fall under divine providence. This would not be possible if everything resulted from the necessity of matter.

9. Evil is the contrary of good. Now, of itself no contrary brings about its contrary, but every contrary brings its contrary to that which is similar to itself. For example, heat does not bring a thing to coldness, except accidentally. Instead, it reduces cold to warmth. Similarly, no good person directs a thing to evil; instead, he directs it to good.

10. As is clear from the above discussion, to do evil is in no way proper to those who are good. To do evil for the sake of a good is blameworthy in a man, and cannot be attributed to God. On the other hand, to direct evil to a good is not opposed to one's goodness. Hence, permitting evil in order to draw some good from it can be attributed to God.

11. [No answer is given to the eleventh difficulty. See the answer to the sixth difficulty of the following article.]

ARTICLE V

In the Fifth Article We Ask: ARE HUMAN ACTS RULED BY PROVIDENCE?

Difficulties:

It seems that they are not, for

1. As Damascene says: "What is in us is the work not of providence but of our own free choice." *What is in us* means our human actions.

Consequently, these do not fall under God' providence.

2. Of the things coming under God's providence, the more noble a thing is, the more elaborately is it provided for. Now, man is more noble than those creatures that lack sensation and, never departing from their course, rarely, if ever, deviate from the right order. Men's actions, however, frequently deviate from the right order. Hence, they are not ruled by providence.

3. The evil of sin is very hateful to God. But no one who is provident permits what is most displeasing to him to happen for the sake of something else, because this would mean that the absence of the latter would be even more displeasing to him. Consequently, since God permits the evil of sin to occur in human acts, it seems that they are not ruled by His providence.

4. What is abandoned does not fall under the rule of providence. But, as we read in Ecclesiasticus (15:14): "God left man in the hand of his own counsel." Human acts, therefore, are not ruled by providence.

5. In Ecclesiastes (9:11) we read: "I saw that . . . the race is not to the swift, nor the battle to the strong . . . but time and chance in all." Since the author is speaking about human acts, it seems that men's actions are subject to the whims of chance and are not ruled by providence.

6. By the rule of providence, different allotments are made to different things. But in

human affairs the same things happen to the good and to the evil; for, as we read in Ecclesiastes (9:2): "All things equally happen to the just and to the wicked, to the good and to the evil." Consequently, human affairs are not ruled by providence.

To the Contrary:

1'. In the Gospel according to Matthew (10:30) is written: "The very hairs of your head are all numbered." Even the least of human acts, therefore, is directed by God's providence.

2'. To punish, reward, and issue commands are acts of providence, because it is through acts of this kind that every provider governs his subjects. Now, God does all these things in connection with human acts. Consequently, all human acts are ruled by His providence.

REPLY:

As pointed out previously, the closer a being is to the first principle, the higher is its place in the order of providence. Now, among all things, spiritual substances stand closest to the first principle; this is why they are said to be stamped with God's image. Consequently, by God's providence they are not only provided for, but they are provident themselves. This is why these substances can exercise a choice in their actions while other creatures cannot. The latter are provided for, but they themselves are not provident.

Now, since providence is concerned with directing to an end, it must take place with the end as its norm; and since the first provider is Himself the end of His providence, He has the norm of providence within Himself. Consequently, it is impossible that any of the failures in those things for which He provides should be due to Him; the failures in these things can be due only to the objects of His providence. Now, creatures to whom His providence has been communicated are not the ends of their own providence. They are directed to another end, namely, God. Hence, it is necessary that they draw the rectitude of their own providence from God's norm. Consequently, in the providence exercised by creatures failures may take place that are due, not only to the objects of their providence, but also to the providers themselves.

However, the more faithful a creature is to the norm of the first provider, the firmer will be the rectitude of his own providence. Consequently, it is because creatures of this sort can fail in their actions and are the cause of their actions, that their failures are culpable—something which is not true of the failures of other creatures. Moreover, because these spiritual creatures are incorruptible even as individuals, they are provided for on their own account as individuals. Hence, defects that take place in them are destined to a reward or punishment which will belong to these individuals themselves—and not to them only as they are ordered to other things.

Now, man is numbered among these creatures, because his form—that is, his soul—is a spiritual being, the root of all his human acts, and that by which even his body has a relation to immortality. Consequently, human acts come under divine providence according as men themselves have providence over their own acts; and the defects in these acts are ordained according to what belongs to these men themselves, not only according to what belongs to others. For example, when a man sins, God orders the sin to the sinner's good, so that after his fall, upon rising again, he may be a more humble person; or it is ordered at least to a good which is brought about in him by divine justice when he is punished for his sin. The defects happening in sensible creatures, however, are directed only to what belongs to others; for example, the corruption of some particular fire is directed to the generation of some particular air. Consequently, to designate this special manner of providence which God exercises over human acts, Wisdom (12:18) says: "Thou with great favour disposest of us."

Answers to Difficulties:

1. The statement of Damascene does not mean that the things in us (that is, in our power to choose) are entirely outside of God's providence, but it means rather that our choice is not determined to one course of action by divine providence, as are the actions of those beings which do not possess freedom.

2. Natural things lacking sensation are provided for by God alone. Consequently, no failure here is possible on the part of the one who provides, but only on the part of the objects of His providence. But human acts can be defective because of human providence. For this reason, we find more failures and deordinations in human acts than we do in the acts of natural things. Yet, the fact that man has providence over his own acts is part of his nobility. Consequently, the number of his failures does not keep man from holding a higher place under God's providence.

3. God loves a thing more if it is a greater good. Consequently, He wills the presence of a greater good more than He wills the absence of a lesser evil (for even the absence of an evil is a certain good). So, in order that certain greater goods may be had, He permits certain persons to fall even into the evils of sin, which, taken as a class, are most hateful, even though one of them may be more hateful to Him than another. Consequently, to cure a man of one sin, God sometimes permits him to fall into another.

4. "God leaves man in the hand of his own counsel" in the sense that He gives him providence over his own acts. Man's providence over his acts, however, does not exclude God's providence over them, just as the active power of creatures does not exclude the active power of God.

5. Even though many of our human acts are

the result of chance if we consider only lower causes, still, if we consider the providence which God has over all things, there is nothing that results from chance. Indeed, the very fact that so many things happen in human affairs when, if we consider merely lower causes, just the opposite should happen, proves that human actions are governed by God's providence. Hence, the powerful frequently fall, for this shows that one is victorious because of God's providence and not because of any human power. The same can be said of other cases.

6. Even though it may seem to us that all things happen equally to the good and to the evil since we are ignorant of the reasons for God's providence in allotting these things, there is no doubt that in all these good and evil things happening to the good or to the evil there is operative a well worked out plan by which God's providence directs all things. It is because we do not know His reasons that we think many things happen without order or plan. We are like a man who enters a carpenter shop and thinks that there is a useless multiplication of tools because he does not know how each one is used; but one who knows the trade will see that this number of tools exists for a very good reason.

ARTICLE VI

In the Sixth Article We Ask: ARE BRUTE ANIMALS AND THEIR ACTS SUBJECT TO GOD'S PROVIDENCE?

Difficulties:

It seems that they are not, for

1. In the first Epistle to the Corinthians (9:9) we read: "Doth God take care for oxen?" Consequently, God does not take care of other animals for the same reason.

2. In the Book of Habacuc (1:14) we read: "Thou wilt make men as the fishes of the sea. . . ." In this passage, the prophet is lamenting the troubling of the order which seems to happen in men's actions. It seems, therefore, that the acts of irrational creatures are not governed by divine providence.

3. If a man is punished for no fault of his own, and this punishment does not help him in any way, it would not seem that human affairs were ruled by providence. Now, brute animals cannot commit a fault, and, when they are killed, their death is not directed to their good, because there is no reward for them after death. Their lives, therefore, are not ruled by providence.

4. A thing is not ruled by God's providence unless it is ordained to the end which He intends; and this end is nothing other than God

Himself. Brutes, however, cannot attain to any participation in God, since they are not capable of beatitude. Consequently, it seems that divine providence does not rule them.

To the Contrary:

1'. In the Gospel according to Matthew (10:29) we read: "not one sparrow shall fall on the ground without our heavenly Father's permission."

2'. Brutes are more noble than creatures that lack sensation. But these other creatures and all their actions come under God's providence. Even more, then, will brutes come under His providence.

REPLY:

In this matter two errors have been made. Some have said that brutes are not ruled by providence except as they participate in the nature of their species, which alone is provided for and directed by God. It is to this kind of providence, they say, that all the passages in Scripture refer when they seem to imply God's providence over brutes, for example: "Who giveth to beasts their food: and to the young . . ." (Psalms 146:9); "The young lions roaring . . ." (Psalms 103:21); and many similar passages. This error, however, attributes a very great imperfection to God. Moreover, it is not possible that God should know the individual acts of brutes and not direct them, since He is most good and, because He is good, pours out His goodness upon all things. Consequently, the error we have mentioned belittles either God's knowledge by denying that He knows individual things or His goodness by denying that He directs individual things as individuals.

For this reason, others have said that the acts of brutes, also, fall under providence in the same way in which the acts of rational beings do. Consequently, no evil would be found in the acts of brutes that would not be directed to their good. This position, however, is also far from reasonable, for punishment and reward is due only to those who have free choice.

It must be said, therefore, that brutes and their acts, taken even individually, fall under God's providence, but not in the same way in which men and their actions do. For providence is exercised over men, even as individuals, for their own sake; but individual brutes are provided for merely for the sake of something else—just as other corruptible creatures are, as mentioned previously. Hence, the evil that happens to a brute is not ordered to the good of the brute but to the good of something else, just as the death of an ass is ordered to the good of a lion or that of a wolf. But the death of a man killed by a lion is directed not merely to the good of the lion, but principally to the man's punishment or to the increase of his merit; for his merit can grow if he accepts his sufferings.

Answers to Difficulties:

1. The Apostle does not intend to remove brutes entirely from God's care. He simply means to say that God does not care so much for brutes that He would impose a law upon men for the sake of brutes, commanding men to be good to them or not to kill them; for brutes have been made for man's use. Consequently, providence is not exercised over them for their own sake but for the sake of men.

2. God has so ordered fishes and brutes that the weak are subject to the strong. This was done without any consideration of merits or demerits, but only for the conservation of the good of nature. The prophet wondered, therefore, if human affairs were governed in the same way. For this to be true, of course, would be unreasonable.

3. A different order of providence is required for human affairs than is required for brutes. Consequently, if the ordering of human affairs were only that proper to brutes, human affairs would seem to be entirely without providence. Yet, that order is sufficient for the providence of brutes.

4. God Himself is the end of all creatures, but in different ways. He is said to be the end of some creatures inasmuch as they participate somewhat in God's image. This participation is common to all creatures. However, He is said to be the end of certain creatures inasmuch as they

can attain God Himself through their own actions. This is the end only of rational creatures, who can know and love God in whom their beatitude lies.

ARTICLE VII

In the Seventh Article We Ask: ARE SINNERS RULED BY GOD'S PROVIDENCE?

Difficulties:

It seems that they are not, for

1. What is left to its own devices is not ruled. But the evil are left to themselves: "So I let them go according to the desires of their heart: they shall walk . . ." (Psalms 80:13). The evil, therefore, are not governed by providence.

2. It is part of the providence by which God rules over men that they are guarded by angels. But guardian angels sometimes abandon men. From their own lips we have these words: "We would have cured Babylon, but she is not healed: let us forsake her. . . ." (Jeremias 51:9). The evil, therefore, are not governed by God's providence.

3. What is given as a reward to the good should not be given to the evil. But government by God is promised as a reward to the good: "The eyes of the Lord are upon the just" (Psalms 33:16).

To the Contrary:

No one justly punishes those who are not under his rule. But God punishes the evil for the sins they commit. Therefore, they are under His rule.

REPLY:

Divine providence extends to men in two ways: first, in so far as men are provided for; second, in so far as they themselves become providers. If they fail in their own providence they are called evil; but if they observe the demands of justice they are called good. Moreover, in so far as they come under providence they are given both good and evil. Now, men are provided for in different ways according to the different ways they have of providing for themselves. For, if they keep the right order in their own providence, God's providence in their regard will keep an ordering that is congruent with their human dignity; that is, nothing will happen to them that is not for their own good, and everything that happens to them will be to their own advantage, according to what is said in the Epistle to the Romans (8:28): "To them that love God, all things work together unto good." However, if in their own providence men do not keep that order which is congruent with their dignity as rational creatures, but provide after the manner of brute animals, then God's providence will dispose of them according to the order that belongs to brutes, so that their good and evil acts will not be directed to their own profit but to the profit of others, according to the words of the Psalmist: "And man when he was in honour did not understand; he is compared . . ." (Psalms 48:13). From this it is evident that God's providence governs the good in a higher way than it governs the evil. For, when the evil leave one order of providence, that is, by not doing the will of God, they fall into another order, an order in which the will of God is done to them. The good, however, are in the true order of His providence in both respects.

Answers to Difficulties:

1. God is said to abandon the wicked, not because they are entirely alien to His providence, but because their acts are not directed to their own profit. This is especially true of the depraved.

2. The angels in charge of guarding men never leave a man entirely. They are merely said to leave a man when, according to God's just judgment, they permit a man to fall into sin or into some punishment.

3. A special kind of providence is promised to the good as a reward. As we mentioned above, this does not belong to the wicked.

ARTICLE VIII

In the Eighth Article We Ask: ARE ALL
MATERIAL CREATURES GOVERNED BY
GOD'S PROVIDENCE THROUGH ANGELS?

Difficulties:

It seems that they are not, for

1. In Job (34:13) we read: "What other hath
he appointed over the earth? or whom hath he
set over the world which he hath made?" In his
commentary on this passage, Gregory says: "By
Himself, indeed, He rules that world who has
created it by Himself." Consequently, God does
not rule material creatures through the mediation of spirits.

2. Damascene says that it is inconsistent to say
that one person makes a thing and another rules
over it. But, without any medium, God alone
creates material creatures. Therefore, He governs
them without any intermediaries.

3. Hugh of St. Victor says that God's providence is His predestination, which is the highest
wisdom and goodness. Now, the highest good or
wisdom is not communicated to any creature.
Therefore, neither is providence. Hence, God
does not provide for material creatures through
the mediation of spiritual creatures.

4. Material creatures are ruled by providence

in so far as they are directed to an end. But bodies are ordained to their end through their natural operations in accordance with their own determinate natures. Therefore, since the natures of natural bodies are made determinate, not by spiritual creatures, but directly by God, it seems that they are not governed through the mediation of spiritual substances.

5. Augustine distinguishes between two types of providential operations: "natural and voluntary." The former he calls natural because it makes trees and plants grow; the latter he calls voluntary because it takes place through the deeds of angels and men. It is clear, therefore, that all material things are ruled by the natural operation of providence, not through the mediation of angels, as would be true were they ruled by voluntary operation.

6. What is attributed to one person because of his dignity does not belong to another who does not have a similar dignity. Now, Jerome writes: "Great is the dignity of souls, each of whom has an angel appointed to guard it." This dignity, however is, not found in material creatures; consequently, they are not committed to the providence and direction of angels.

7. The effects and due courses of these material bodies are frequently hindered. This would not happen if they were governed by the mediation of angels, because these obstacles would then occur either with the consent of the angels— and this is impossible, since it would be contrary

to that for which angels were appointed, namely, the government of natures according to its due order—or they would occur against the angels' will—and this, too, is impossible, since the angels would not be in the state of beatitude if something could happen to them which they did not want to happen. Therefore, material creatures are not ruled through the mediation of spiritual creatures.

8. The more noble and powerful a cause is, the more perfect is its effect. Now, lower causes can produce such effects as can be kept in existence even after the operation of their efficient cause ceases; for example, a knife continues in existence even after the work of the cutler has ceased. Much more so, then, will the effects of God's power be able to exist by themselves without being provided for by any efficient cause. Consequently, they do not need to be ruled through angels.

9. The divine goodness has created the whole world in order to manifest itself; for, as we read in Proverbs (16:4): "The Lord hath made all things for himself. . . ." Now, God's goodness, as Augustine also says, is manifested more by a diversity of natures than by a number of things all possessing the same nature. For this reason, God did not make all creatures rational or all of them to exist in themselves. He made some creatures irrational, and some, like accidents, that exist in others. Consequently, it seems that for the greater manifestation of Himself God created

not only creatures that needed the rule of another, but also some creatures that needed no rule at all. Hence, our position stands.

10. There are two types of acts in creatures, first act and second act. First act is the form and the act of existence that a form gives. Form is called the *primarily first* act, existence, the *secondarily first* act. Second act, however, is operation. Now, the first act of corporeal things comes directly from God. Therefore, their second acts are also caused directly by God. But the only way in which one thing governs another is by being in some manner the cause of its operations. Therefore, material creatures of this sort are not governed through the instrumentality of spirits.

11. According to Augustine, God simultaneously created a world that was perfect in all its parts in order that His power might be better shown. The praiseworthiness of His providence would similarly be even better shown if He were to govern all things directly. Therefore, He does not govern material things through the mediation of spirits.

12. There are two ways of governing. One way is to impart light or knowledge; this is the way in which a teacher rules his class, and a ruler, his city. The other way is to impart motion to a thing; this is the way in which a pilot guides his ship. Now, spiritual creatures do not govern material creatures by imparting light or knowledge, because these material things cannot receive knowledge, nor do they govern them by

imparting motion, because, as is proved in the *Physics,* a mover must be joined to what he moves, and spiritual substances are not joined to these lesser material bodies. Consequently, the latter are not governed in any way through their mediation.

13. Boethius says: "Through Himself alone God disposes all things." His disposition of material things, therefore, does not take place through spirits.

To the Contrary:

1'. Gregory says: "In this visible world, nothing can be disposed except through invisible creatures."

2'. Augustine writes: "All material things are ruled in a definite order through the spirit of life."

3'. Augustine also says: "God does certain things Himself, as illuminating and beatifying souls. Other things He does through creatures who serve Him. These, in proportion to their merit and according to inviolable laws, are ordained to care even for sparrows, even for the beauty of the grass of the fields, indeed, even for the number of hairs on our heads—and to all this divine providence extends." Now, the creatures ordained to serve God's inviolable decrees are the angels; consequently, it is through them that He governs material things.

4'. Origen writes: "The world needs the angels, who rule over beasts, preside over the birth of animals, and over the growth of bushes, plants, and other things."

5'. Hugh of St. Victor says: "The ministry of angels rules not only over the life of men but also over the things that are related to their life." Now, all material things are ordained for men's use. Consequently, all things are governed through the mediation of angels.

6'. In a co-ordinated series, the earlier members act on the later members. The later do not act on the earlier. But spiritual substances are prior to material, since they are closer to the first principle. Therefore, the action of spiritual substances governs material actions, and the opposite is not true.

7'. Man is said to be a "microcosm" because the soul rules the human body as God rules the whole universe. In this respect, the soul is called "an image of God" more than angels are. Now, our soul governs the body through the mediation of certain spirits which are spiritual in comparison with the body, although material in comparison with the soul. Consequently, God also rules material creatures through the mediation of spiritual creatures.

8'. Our soul exercises certain operations directly, for example, understanding and willing; but it exercises other operations mediately by using bodily organs as instruments, as, for example, in the operations of the sensitive and vegetative soul. God also exercises certain operations directly, such as the beatifying of souls and the other actions He performs in relation to the highest substances. Consequently, some of God's operations will also take place in the lowest substances through the mediation of the highest ones.

9'. The first cause does not take away the operation of a second cause, but, as is clear from what is said in *The Causes,* it strengthens it. Now, if God were to govern all things immediately, second causes would have no operations of their own. God, therefore, rules lower beings through higher beings.

10'. In the universe there is something, such as the ultimate constituents of bodies, which is ruled but does not rule. There is something, such as God, which is not ruled but rules. Therefore, there will exist something that both rules and is ruled—a medium between both types. Consequently, God rules lower creatures through the mediation of higher.

REPLY:

As Dionysius and Augustine say, the divine goodness is the cause of things' being brought into existence, for God wished to communicate His goodness to others as far as this was possible to creatures. God's goodness, however, has a twofold perfection. We can consider it in itself as it contains all perfections in itself in a supereminent way, or we can consider it as it flows into things, that is, as it is the cause of things. It was fitting, therefore, that God's divine goodness should be communicated to creatures in both ways so that because of this goodness created things not only would exist and possess goodness but also would give existence and goodness to other things, just like the sun's outpoured rays, which not only illumine other bodies but also make them to be sources of light, too. However, the following order is kept: Those that most resemble the sun receive the most of its light and, consequently, have sufficient light not only for themselves but also to pour out on other things.

Similarly, in the ordering of the universe, as a result of the outpouring of God's goodness, superior creatures have not only that by which they are good in themselves, but also that by which they are the cause of goodness for other things which participate the least in God's goodness. These last-named things participate in the divine goodness merely in order to exist—not to be the cause of other things. And this is the reason, as Augustine and the Philosopher say, why that which is active is always more noble than that which is passive.

Now, among the superior creatures, the closest to God are those rational ones that exist, live, and understand in the likeness of God. Consequently, God in His goodness gives them the power not only of pouring out upon other things but also of having the same manner of outpouring that He Himself has—that is, according to their will, and not according to any necessity of their nature. Hence, God governs inferior creatures both through spiritual creatures and through the more noble material creatures. He provides through material creatures, not by making them provident themselves, but by making them active. He governs through spiritual creatures, however, by making them provident themselves.

But even in rational creatures an order can be found. Rational souls hold the lowest place among these, and their light is shadowy in comparison with that of the angels. Consequently, as Dionysius says, their knowledge is more restricted, and their providence is likewise restricted to a few things, namely, to human affairs and practical matters of human life. But the providence of angels is universal and extends to all material creation. Consequently, both saints and philosophers say that all corporeal things are governed by divine providence through the mediation of angels. We must differ with the philosophers, however, in this, that some of them say that corporeal things are not only cared for by angels but are also created by them. This opinion is contrary to faith. We should follow, instead, the opinion of the saints who hold that corporeal things of this sort are administered by the providence of angels through motion only; that is, the angels move the higher bodies, and these motions cause the motions of the lower.

Answers to Difficulties:

1. An exclusive statement regarding an agent does not exclude the operation of an instrument; it merely excludes another principal agent. Hence, if one were to say, "Socrates alone makes a knife," not the operation of his hammer but only the operation of another carpenter is excluded. Similarly, when it is said that God governs the world by Himself, this does not exclude the operation of inferior causes, which God uses as instrumental means. All that is excluded is government by another principal ruler.

2. The governing of a thing pertains to its direction to an end. The ordination of a thing to an end, however, presupposes its act of existing; but its act of existing presupposes nothing else. Consequently, creation, by which all things are brought into existence, is the operation of the only cause that presupposes no other cause by which it is kept in existence. Government, however, can be one of those causes that do presuppose other causes, so it is not necessary for God to create through the mediation of certain causes through whose instrumentality He governs.

3. What creatures receive from God cannot exist in them in the same manner in which it exists in Him. Consequently, this difference becomes apparent when names are applied to Him. Those names that express some perfection absolutely are common also to creatures; but those that express both a perfection and its manner

of existing in God are not common to creatures, for example, *omnipotence, supreme wisdom,* and *supreme goodness.* It is clear, therefore, that even though supreme goodness is not communicated to a creature, providence can be communicated to it.

4. Even though that establishment of nature by which material things receive a tendency to an end comes directly from God, their motion and action can take place through the instrumentality of angels, just as natures in seeds possess their undeveloped nature from God alone but, by the providence of a farmer, are helped to develop into act. Consequently, just as a farmer supervises the growth of the crops in his fields, so do angels direct the entire activity of material creation.

5. Augustine divides the operation of natural providence from that of voluntary providence by considering the proximate principles of their operations; and nature is the proximate principle of some operations of divine providence, while the will is that of others. But the remote principle of all providential action is the will, at least the divine will. The argument, therefore, proves nothing.

6. Just as all material bodies lie under God's providence but God's care is nevertheless said to be only for men because of the special kind of providence He has for them, so also, even though all material bodies are subject to the rule of angels, nevertheless, because of the dignity of

men's souls, angels are appointed to guard men in a very special way.

7. Just as the will of God as a ruler is not opposed to defects in things but, instead, allows or permits them, so is the same entirely true of the wills of angels, which are perfectly conformed to the divine will.

8. As Avicenna says, no effect can remain if its proper cause is removed. Now, certain inferior causes are causes of becoming; others are causes of existing. A cause of becoming is that which educes a form from the potentiality of matter by means of motion, such as a cutler who is the efficient cause of a knife. A cause of a thing's existing, however, is that upon which the act of existence of a thing essentially depends, as the existence of light in the air depends upon the sun. Now, if the cutler is removed, the becoming of the knife ceases, but not its existence. However, if the sun is taken away, there ceases the very existence of the light in the air. Similarly, if God's action ceases, the existence of a creature utterly ceases, since God is the cause not only of a thing's becoming but also of its existence.

9. That condition cannot possibly be in a creature; that is, a creature cannot have an act of existence without someone keeping it in that act. It is repugnant to the very notion of a creature; for a creature, because it is a creature, has an act of existence that is caused, and, consequently, it depends on something else.

10. More things are required for second act than for first act. Hence, it is not unreasonable that something should be the cause of another's motion and operation, even though it is not the cause of its act of existence.

11. The breadth of God's providence and goodness is manifested more clearly in His governance of inferior beings through superior beings than if He were to govern all things directly. For in this kind of government, as is clear from what has been said, the perfection of God's goodness is communicated in more than one regard.

12. A spiritual creature governs a material one by giving it motion. This does not necessitate that spiritual creatures be joined to all bodies, but only to those which they move directly, namely, the first bodies. Spiritual creatures, moreover, are not joined to these bodies by being their forms, as some have held, but by being their movers.

13. When something is said to take place through another, the preposition *through* implies that it is a cause of the operation. Now, since an operation stands halfway between the one doing the work and the work that is done *through* can imply a cause of the operation in so far as this cause issues in a result. In this sense it is said that something takes place *through* an instrument. *Through* can also, however, signify a cause of the operation in so far as the operation comes from the one operating. In this sense we say that something takes place *through* the form

of the agent. Now, here it is not the instrument which is the cause of the agent's action, but his form or some superior agent is the cause. However, an instrument can be the cause of the result which receives the agent's action.

Consequently, when we read that God disposes all things through Himself alone, *through* denotes the cause of His divine disposition in so far as it comes from God who is disposing. In this sense, God is said to dispose through Himself alone, because He is not moved by any superior disposing Him; and He disposes, not through any extrinsic form, but only through His own goodness.

ARTICLE IX

In the Ninth Article We Ask: Does Divine
Providence Dispose Bodies Here Below
by Means of the Celestial Bodies?

Difficulties:

It seems not, for

1. Speaking of celestial bodies, Damascene writes as follows: "We say, however, that they do not cause generation or corruption." Since bodies here below are subject to generation and corruption, they are consequently not disposed through celestial bodies.

2. It was said, however, that the celestial

bodies are not called the causes of bodies here
below merely because they do not introduce any
necessity into them. On the contrary, if an
effect of a heavenly body on bodies here below is
impeded, this must have been caused by some
condition in the lower bodies. Now, if the lower
bodies are ruled by the heavenly bodies, then
that obstructing condition must be traced to
some influence of a heavenly body. Consequently,
no impediment could arise from bodies here below unless it were due to an exigency of the
celestial bodies. Therefore, if the celestial bodies
rule the lower, and if the motions of the celestial
bodies are necessary, they will introduce necessity into the lower bodies.

3. For an action to be completed, all that is
needed is something active and something
passive. Now, both active and passive natural
powers are found in bodies here below. Therefore, no power of a celestial body is needed for
their actions. Consequently, bodies here below
are not ruled through the instrumentality of
celestial bodies.

4. According to Augustine, there are three
types of things: first, things that are acted upon
but do not act (e.g., bodies); second, things that
act but are not acted upon (e.g., God); third,
things that both act and are acted upon (e.g.,
spiritual substances). Now, celestial bodies are
simply corporeal. Consequently, they do not
have the power of acting upon bodies here be-

low. Hence, the latter are not disposed through their instrumentality.

5. If a celestial body acts upon bodies here below, either it acts upon them in so far as it is a body, that is, through its material form, or it acts upon them through something else. Now, a celestial body does not act in so far as it is a body, because this kind of action can be found in all bodies; and this explanation seems unlikely from what Augustine says. Consequently, if it does act upon lower bodies, its action is due to something else; and, in this case, it should be attributed to an immaterial power and not to the heavenly bodies. Hence, the conclusion is the same as before.

6. What does not belong to what is prior does not belong to what is subsequent. Now, as the Commentator says, material forms presuppose indeterminate dimensions in matter. However, dimensions are not active, because quantity is not an active principle. Therefore, material forms are not active principles, and so no body can do anything except through an immaterial power existing within it. Consequently, the conclusion is the same as before.

7. Explaining this statement made in *The Causes,* "Every noble soul has three operations," a commentator declares that the soul acts on nature by means of a divine power existing within it. A soul, however, is much more noble than a body. Hence, neither can a body do any-

thing to the soul except by means of a divine power within it. Consequently, our original position stands.

8. That which is more simple is not moved by what is less simple. But seminal principles in the matter of bodies here below are more simple than the material power of the heavens, because the power of the latter is diffused in matter while that of the seminal principles is not. Therefore, the seminal principles in bodies here below cannot be moved by the power of a celestial body. Hence, bodies here below are not governed in their motions by celestial bodies.

9. Augustine writes as follows: "Nothing pertains to the body more than the body's sex. Yet, twins of different sexes can be conceived when the stars are in the same position." Therefore, celestial bodies have no influence even on material things, and our original position stands.

10. As we read in *The Causes:* "The first cause has more effect on what is caused by a second cause than the second cause itself has." Now, if bodies here below are disposed by celestial bodies, then with respect to the powers in bodies here below the powers of the celestial bodies are in a relation similar to that of the first cause; and the powers in bodies here below are then like second causes. Hence, effects taking place in bodies here below are determined more by the disposition of the celestial spheres than they are by the powers of the bodies themselves. However, there is necessity in the celestial bodies,

since they always remain the same. Therefore, their effects below will also be necessary. But this is not true. Consequently, the first statement —that bodies here below are disposed by heavenly bodies—is also not true.

11. As we read in *The Heavens,* the motion of the heavens is natural. Consequently, it can hardly be voluntary or the result of a choice. The things that are caused by it, therefore, are not caused as the result of a choice, and so do not come under providence. It would be unreasonable, however, to suppose that bodies here below are not governed by providence. Therefore, it is unreasonable for the motion of celestial bodies to be the cause of bodies here below.

12. When a cause is placed, an effect is placed. Therefore, the act of existence of a cause is, as it were, antecedent to that of an effect. Now, if an antecedent is necessary, the consequent is also necessary. Therefore, if a cause is necessary, the effect is likewise necessary. However, the effects taking place in bodies here below are not necessary but contingent. Consequently, they are not caused by the motion of the heavens, which is necessary because natural. Therefore, our original position stands.

13. The final cause of a thing's becoming is more noble than the thing. But all things were made for the sake of man—even heavenly bodies. For we read the following in Deuteronomy (4:19): "Lest perhaps lifting up thy eyes to heaven, thou see the sun and the moon, and all

the stars of heaven, and being deceived by error thou adore them, which the Lord thy God created for the service of all the nations that are under heaven." Therefore, man is more noble than the celestial bodies. Now, what is less noble does not influence what is more noble. Consequently, celestial bodies have no influence on a human body, and, for the same reason, none on other bodies such as elements that are prior to the human body.

14. It was said, however, that man is more noble than the heavenly bodies because of his soul, not because of his body. On the contrary, a nobler perfection is proper to a nobler subject. Now, the body of a man has a more noble form than a heavenly body has; for the form of the heavens is purely material, and a rational soul is much more noble than matter. Therefore, even the body of a man is nobler than a heavenly body.

15. A contrary is not the cause of its contrary. Now, occasionally, the power of a celestial body is opposed to the introduction of certain effects into lower bodies. For example, sometimes a celestial body starts to cause dampness, while a doctor is trying to dispose of some matter by drying it up in order to restore health; and he often succeeds in doing this even though a heavenly body is exerting a contrary influence. Therefore, heavenly bodies do not cause physical effects in bodies here below.

16. Since all action takes place through con-

tact, what makes no contact does not act. Heavenly bodies, however, do not touch bodies here below. Consequently, they do not act upon them; and the original position stands.

17. But it was said that heavenly bodies contact lower bodies through a medium.—On the contrary, whenever there is contact and action through a medium, the medium must receive the effect of the agent before the end-term does. For example, fire heats the air before it heats us. Now, the effects of the sun and of the stars cannot be received in the lower spheres because these have the nature of the fifth essence and consequently cannot be affected by heat, cold, or any of the other states found in bodies here below. Therefore, no action can come from the heavenly bodies through the lower spheres to bodies here below.

18. Providence is communicated to what is an instrument of providence. But providence cannot be communicated to heavenly bodies, since they lack intelligence. Therefore, they cannot be an instrument for providing for things.

To the Contrary:

1′. Augustine says: "Bodies with weaker and grosser natures are ruled in a definite order by those that are more subtle and powerful." Now, the heavenly bodies are more subtle and powerful than bodies here below. Therefore, they rule the bodies here below.

2′. Dionysius says that the rays of the sun "enable visible bodies to generate and give them life, nourishment, and growth." Now, these are the more noble effects to be found in bodies here below. Consequently, all the other physical effects also are produced by the providence of God through the mediation of celestial bodies.

3'. According to the Philosopher, that which is first in any genus is the cause of the others that come afterwards in that genus. But the heavenly bodies are first in the genus of bodies, and their motions are first of all material motions. They are, therefore, the cause of material bodies that are moved here below. Hence, the conclusion is the same as before.

4'. According to the Philosopher, the movement of the sun along an inclined circle causes generation and corruption in bodies here below. Consequently, generations and corruptions are measured by this movement. Aristotle also says that all the variety found in concepts is due to the heavenly bodies. Therefore, bodies here below are disposed through their mediation.

5'. Rabbi Moses says that the heavens are in the universe as a heart is in an animal. But all the other members are ruled by the soul through the instrumentality of the heart. Therefore, all material things are ruled by God through the instrumentality of the heavens.

REPLY:

The common intention of all philosophers was to reduce multitude to unity and variety to uniformity as much as possible. Consequently, after considering the diversity of actions to be found in bodies here below, the ancient philosophers attempted to reduce these bodies to some fewer and more simple principles, that is, to elements, one or many, and to elementary qualities. But their position is not logical; for, in the actions of natural things, elementary qualities are like instrumental principles. An indication of this is the fact that they do not have the same way of acting in all things, nor do their actions always arrive at the same term. They have different effects in gold, in wood, and in the flesh of an animal. Now, this would not happen unless their actions were controlled by something else. Moreover, the action of the principal agent is not reduced to the action of an instrument as to its principle. Rather, the opposite is true, as, for example, a product of handicraft ought not be attributed to the saw but to the craftsman. Therefore, neither can natural effects be reduced to elementary qualities as to their first principles.

Consequently, others (the Platonists) made simple and separated forms the first principles of natural effects. These were the origin, they said, of the existence, generation, and every natural property of bodies here below. This opinion also, however, is false; for, if a cause remains always the same, then the effect is always the same. Now, the forms they posited were immovable. Consequently, any generation resulting from them would always have to happen in bodies here below in a constant manner. But we see with our own eyes that what happens is quite the contrary.

It is therefore necessary to say that in bodies here below the principles of generation, of corruption, and of the other motions that depend upon these do not always remain the same; but they nevertheless always remain as the first principles of generation, and thereby make continual generation possible. Moreover, they must be unchangeable in their substance, and subject only to local motion. Consequently, as a result of their approach or withdrawal, they bring about diverse and contrary motions in bodies here below. Now, the heavenly bodies are of just such a nature. Consequently, all material effects should be reduced to them as to their cause.

In this reduction, however, two errors have been made. Some have reduced the bodies here below to heavenly bodies, as though the latter were their absolute first cause, for these philosophers denied that immaterial substances exist. Consequently, they said that what is prior among bodies is first among beings. This, however, is clearly false. Whatever is moved must be reduced to a first immovable principle, since nothing is moved by itself, and one cannot keep going back into infinity. Now, even though a heavenly body does not undergo change by generation or corruption or by a motion which would alter what belongs to its substance, it is nevertheless moved locally. Consequently, the reduction must be made to some prior principle so that things un-

dergoing qualitative change are traced back by a
definite order to that which causes this change in
other things but is not so changed itself, although it is moved locally; and then further back
to that which does not change in any way at all.

Others have asserted that the heavenly bodies
cause not only the motion of bodies here below
but also their very beginning. For example,
Avicenna says that, as a result of what is common to all heavenly bodies, that is, their circular
motion, there is caused the common element of
bodies here below, namely, first matter; and, as
a result of those things which differentiate one
heavenly body from another, there is caused the
difference in their forms. Thus, the heavenly
bodies are media, to some extent, between God
and things here below even in the line of creation. This position, however, is contrary to faith,
which teaches that the whole of nature in its
first beginning was created directly by God. But
that one creature should be moved by another,
presupposing that natural powers of each creature are given it as a result of God's work, is not
contrary to faith. Consequently, we say that the
heavenly bodies are the causes of bodies here
below merely in the line of motion. Thus, these
heavenly bodies are instruments in the work of
governing, but not in the work of creating.

Answers to Difficulties:

1. Damascene intends to exclude from heavenly bodies only first causality or any causality

which would introduce necessity into bodies here below. For, even if heavenly bodies always act in the same way, their effects are received in lower bodies according to the manner of these lower bodies, which are frequently seen to be in a contrary state. Consequently, the forces exercised by the heavenly bodies are not always able to bring about their effects in the bodies here below, because a contrary disposition prevents them from doing so. This is why the Philosopher says that signs of storms and winds frequently appear, but the storms and winds do not take place because the contrary dispositions are stronger.

2. Those dispositions that resist the force of the celestial bodies are caused in the original creation, not by a heavenly body, but by God's operation, which has made fire to be hot, water to be cold, and so forth. Consequently, we should not reduce all impediments of this kind to the celestial bodies.

3. The active powers in these lower bodies are merely instrumental. Consequently, like an instrument which does not move unless it is moved by a first agent, the active powers of inferior bodies cannot operate unless moved by celestial bodies.

4. That objection touches a certain opinion found in *The Fount of Life,* to the effect that no body acts because of any power that it has as a body, because the quantity found in matter prevents the form from acting. Hence, every action **we** attribute to a body is really the action of

some spiritual power operating in it. According to Rabbi Moses, this opinion was held by certain teachers among the Moors who said that fire does not heat, but God heats in the fire. This position, however, is foolish, since it denies all things their natural operations. Moreover, it is contrary to what philosophers and saints have said. Consequently, we say that bodies act by means of their material power; nevertheless, God operates in all things as a first cause operating in a second cause.

Therefore, the statement made to the effect that bodies are only acted upon but do not act should be understood in this sense: only that is said to act which has dominion over its action. It was in this sense that Damascene asserted: "Brute animals do not act but are only acted upon." But this does not mean that animals do not act if *act* is taken to mean simply the performance of an action.

5. As we read in *Generation and Corruption,* that which is active is always other than or contrary to that which is passive. Consequently, it does not belong to a body to act upon another body with respect to that which it has in common with that body, but only with respect to that in which it is different from it. A body, therefore, does not act in so far as it is a body, but in so far as it is a certain kind of body. For example, no animal reasons inasmuch as it is simply animal, but some animals reason inasmuch as they are also men. Similarly, fire does not heat in so far as it is a body, but in so far as

it is hot. The same is true of a celestial body.

6. Before the advent of natural forms, dimensions are presupposed as existing in matter in a state of incomplete act, not of complete act. Consequently, they are first in the line of matter and of generation. Form, however, is first in the line of completion. Now, a thing acts in so far as it is completed and is an actual being, not in so far as it is in potency. As a being in potency it is merely passive. Hence, it does not follow from the fact that matter or dimensions pre-existing in matter are not active that form is likewise inactive. Instead, the opposite follows. It would follow, however, if these dimensions were not passive, that the form would not be passive. But, as the Commentator says, the form of a heavenly body is not in it through the mediation of dimensions of the sort described.

7. The order of effects should correspond to the order of causes. According to the author of that book, however, the following order of causes exists: first, the first cause, God; second, the intelligence; third, the soul. Consequently, the first effect, the act of existence, is properly attributed to the first cause; the second effect, knowing, is attributed to intelligence; the third effect, moving, is attributed to the soul.

A second cause, however, always acts in virtue of the first cause, and, consequently, possesses something of its operation (like the lower spheres which possess something of the motion of the highest). According to the author, however, the intelligence not only knows but also gives existence; and the soul, which he holds to be caused by the intelligence, has not only the motion of the soul, which is to move, but also that of an intellect, which is to understand, and that of God, which is to give existence. I admit these to be the actions of a noble soul, but he understands such a soul to be the soul of a heavenly body or any other rational soul whatsoever.

Therefore, it is not necessary that the divine power be the only one to move all things without any intermediary. The lower causes can also move through their own powers in so far as they participate in the power of superior causes.

8. According to Augustine, seminal principles are all the active and passive powers given to creatures by God; and through their instrumentality natural effects are brought into existence. He writes in *The Trinity:* "Like a mother pregnant with her unborn infant, the world is pregnant with the causes of unborn things." While explaining what he said above about seminal principles, he also called them "the powers and faculties" that are allotted to things.

Consequently, included in these seminal principles are the active powers of celestial bodies, which are more noble than the active powers of bodies here below and, consequently, able to move them. They are called seminal principles inasmuch as all effects are originally in their active causes in the manner of seeds. But if, as some hold, seminal principles are understood as being the beginnings of forms in first matter, inasmuch as first matter is in potency to all forms, then, even though this does not agree very much with the words of Augustine, it can be said that the simplicity of these principles, like the simplicity of first matter, is caused by their imperfection, and, because of it, they cannot be moved, just as first matter cannot be.

9. Differentiation of the sexes must be attributed to celestial causes. Our reason for saying this is as follows: Every agent tends to form to its own likeness, as far as possible, that which is passive in its respect. Accordingly, the active principle in the male seed always tends toward the generation of a male offspring, which is more perfect than the female. From this it follows that conception of female offspring is something of an accident in the order of nature—in so far, at least, as it is not the result of the natural causality of the particular agent. Therefore, if there were no other natural influence at work tending toward the conception of female offspring, such conception would be wholly outside the design of nature, as is the case with what we call "monstrous" births. And so it is said that, although the conception of female offspring is not the natural result of the efficient causality of the particular nature at work—for which reason the female is sometimes spoken of as an "accidental male"—nevertheless, the con-

ception of female offspring is the natural result
of universal nature; that is, it is due to the influence of a heavenly body, as Avicenna sug-
gests.

Matter, however, can cause an impediment
which will prevent both the celestial force and
the particular nature from attaining their effect,
namely, the production of a male. And so, sometimes, as a result of an improper disposition in
matter, a female is conceived even when the
celestial influence tends to the contrary; or the
opposite may happen, and, despite the influence
of the celestial body, a male will sometimes be
conceived because the formative influence of the
particular agent is strong enough to overcome
the defect in the material. In the conception of
twins, the matter is separated by the operation
of nature; and one part of the matter yields to
the active principle more than the other part
does because of the latter's deficiency. Consequently, in one part a female is generated, in
the other, a male—independently of the dispositions of the celestial spheres one way or the
other. The generation of a female twin, however, happens more often when a celestial body
disposes to the female sex.

10. A first cause is said to have more influence
than a second cause in so far as its effect is
deeper and more permanent in what is caused
than the effect of the second cause is. Nevertheless, the effect has more resemblance to the second cause, since the action of the first cause is

in some way determined to this particular effect by means of the second cause.

11. Although a movement in the heavens, as it is the act of a movable body, is not a voluntary motion, nevertheless, as it is the act of a mover, it is voluntary; that is to say, it is caused by a will. And in this respect the things which are caused by this movement may come under providence.

12. An effect does not follow from a first cause unless the second cause has already been placed. Consequently, the necessity of a first cause does not introduce necessity into its effect unless the second cause is also necessary.

13. The celestial bodies are not made for man in the sense that man is their principal end. Their principal end is the divine goodness. Moreover, that man is nobler than a heavenly body is not due to the nature of his body but to the nature of his rational soul. Besides, even granting that man's body were, speaking absolutely, nobler than a celestial body, this would not prevent a celestial body from being nobler than a human body under a certain aspect, namely, as it has active power while the latter has merely passive power; and in this respect, a celestial body can act upon the human body. Similarly, fire as it is actually hot can act upon a human body in so far as the latter is potentially hot.

14. The rational soul is a substance as well as the act of a body. As a substance, therefore, it is nobler than the form of a celestial body;

but it is not nobler as the act of a body. Or it could be said that the soul is a perfection of the human body both as a form and as a mover. But, since a celestial body is more perfect, it does not need a spiritual substance to perfect it as a form, but only to perfect it as a mover. This self-sufficiency makes it naturally more noble than [man who needs] a human soul.

Even though some have asserted that the movers of the heavenly spheres are joined to them as forms, Augustine left the matter in doubt. In his commentary on the words of Ecclesiastes (1:6), "The spirit goeth forward surveying all places round about," Jerome seems to follow the affirmative position; for he says: "He calls the sun a spirit because it breathes and lives like an animal." Damascene, however, holds the contrary: "Let no one think that the heavens or the stars are living. They lack both life and feeling."

15. Even the action of a contrary which resists the active influence of a celestial body has some cause in the heavens; for, as the philosophers say, things here below are sustained in their actions by the first motion. Consequently, a contrary whose action impedes the effect of a celestial body, like the hot remedy which impedes moistening by the moon, nevertheless has a cause in the heavens. Similarly, the health that follows is not entirely contrary to the action of the celestial body but has some roots there.

16. As is said in *Generation and Corruption*, heavenly bodies contact bodies here below, but

are not contacted by them. Moreover, as was mentioned, no heavenly body immediately contacts a body here below. The contact is through a medium.

17. The action of the agent is received in the medium according to the manner of the medium. Consequently, it is sometimes received in a different way in the medium than in the ultimate term. For example, the force of a magnet attracting iron passes to the iron through the medium of air, which is not attracted; and, as the Commentator says, the force of a fish that shocks the hand is transmitted to the hand through a net which is not shocked. Moreover, heavenly bodies do have all the qualities found in bodies below, but in their own way (which is that of a source) and not as in these lower bodies. Consequently, their actions are not received in the intermediate spheres in such a way that these are changed as the lower bodies are.

18. Bodies of this kind here below are ruled by divine providence through the higher bodies, but not in such a way that divine providence is communicated to them. They are made merely the instruments by which God's providence is carried out—just as art is not communicated to a hammer, which is merely an instrument of the art.

ARTICLE X

In the Tenth Article We Ask: ARE HUMAN ACTS
GOVERNED BY GOD'S PROVIDENCE THROUGH THE
INSTRUMENTALITY OF CELESTIAL BODIES?

Difficulties:

It seems that they are, for

1. According to Damascene, heavenly bodies
"are responsible for our habits, temperament,
and disposition." Now, habits and dispositions
belong to the intellect and the will, which are
the principles of human acts. Consequently, human acts are disposed by God through the mediation of celestial bodies.

2. We read in *The Six Principles:* "That the
soul when joined to a body, imitates the temperament of that body." But, since the celestial
bodies leave their impression on a man's temperament, they thereby influence his soul. Hence,
they can cause human acts.

3. Whatever acts upon a prior member of a
series also acts upon a subsequent member. Now,
the essence of the soul exists before its powers
of intellect and will exist, because these have
their origin in the essence of the soul. Therefore, since the celestial bodies leave their impression on the essence of the rational soul, which
they do inasmuch as the soul is the act of a body

—a function belonging to it by its very essence, it seems that they leave their impression on the intellect and will, and, consequently, are principles of human acts.

4. An instrument acts, not only because of its own power, but also because of the power of the principal agent. Now, since a heavenly body is a moved mover, it is the instrument of the spiritual substance moving it. Consequently, its motion is not that of a body alone but it is also the act of the spirit moving it. Therefore, its motion takes place, not only by reason of the body moved, but also by reason of the spirit moving it. Now, just as that celestial body is superior to a human body, so is that spiritual substance superior to a human spirit. Consequently, that motion leaves its impression on a man's soul as well as on his body. It seems, therefore, that they are the principles of his acts of intellect and will.

5. By experience we know that from their birth some men have talents for learning or exercising certain crafts. Hence, some become carpenters, others become doctors, and so forth. Now, this proclivity cannot be reduced to the proximate principles of generation as its cause, for children are often found to have a bent to certain things which their parents did not have. This difference in talent, therefore, should be reduced to the celestial bodies as its cause. Moreover, it cannot be said that this sort of talent is in men's souls through the mediation of their

bodies, because the physical qualities of the body do not contribute to these inclinations as they actually do to anger, joy, and similar passions of the soul. Celestial bodies, therefore, leave their impression on men's souls immediately and directly. Consequently, human acts are disposed through the instrumentality of the celestial bodies.

6. Of all human acts, the following seem to be superior to all others: ruling, waging wars, and similar actions. But, as Isaac says: "God made a sphere to rule over kingdoms and wars." Much more, then, are other human acts disposed through the mediation of heavenly bodies.

7. It is easier to transfer a part than a whole. But, according to philosophers, the influence of the celestial bodies sometimes moves the entire population of a province to launch a war. Much more, then, can the power of these celestial bodies affect some particular man.

To the Contrary:

1′. Damascene writes of the heavenly bodies that they never cause our acts: "We have been given free choice by our Maker, and we are the masters of our conduct."

2′. Both Augustine and Gregory support this contrary view.

REPLY:

To get a clear understanding of this question, we must first understand what is meant by *hu-*

man acts. Human acts, properly speaking, are those over which a man is master. A man, however, is the master of his acts through his will or free choice. Consequently, this question is concerned with the acts of the will and of free choice. There are, of course, other acts in man that do not lie under the command of his will, for example, the acts of his nutritive and generative powers. These acts lie under the influence of celestial forces, just as other physical acts do.

There have been many errors regarding human acts. Some have said that human acts do not come under God's providence and cannot be reduced to any cause other than our own providence. As Augustine says, this seems to have been the position of Cicero. The position, however, is untenable; for, as proved in *The Soul,* our will is a moved mover. Consequently, its act must be reduced to some first principle that is an unmoved mover.

For this reason, some have reduced all the acts of the will to the celestial bodies; for, since they asserted that our senses and intellect are the same, it followed that all the powers of the soul are material and, therefore, subject to the action of the heavenly bodies. The Philosopher, however, destroys this position by showing that the intellect is an immaterial power and that its action is not material. As he says in *The Generation of Animals,* if the actions of principles are immaterial, the principles themselves must

be immaterial. Consequently, it is impossible for
the actions of the will and intellect of themselves to be reduced to any material principles.

Avicenna, therefore, declared that heavenly
bodies were made, like man, of a soul and body,
and that, just as the actions and motion of a
human body are reduced to celestial bodies, so
all the actions of the soul are reduced to celestial souls as to their principles. Consequently,
whatever will we have is caused by the will of
a celestial soul. This position is consistent with
his opinion on the end of man, which he holds
to be the union of the human soul with a celestial soul or intelligence. For, since the perfection
of the will is its end and its good—and this is
its object, just as the visible is the object of
sight—then that which acts upon the will should
have the nature of an end, because an efficient
cause acts only in so far as it impresses its form
on a recipient.

Faith, however, teaches that God is the direct
end of man's life, and that we will be beatified
and enjoy the vision of God. Consequently, He
alone can leave an impression on our will. Now,
the order of what is moved should correspond
to the order of the movers. But in our ordination to our end, with which providence is concerned, the first thing that is in us is our will;
and the characters of the good and of an end
primarily pertain to the will, which uses everything we have as instruments toward achieving
our end. However, in a certain respect the in-

tellect precedes the will, and is, moreover, more closely related to it than our bodily powers are. Consequently, God alone, who is the first provider in all respects, leaves His imprint on our will; the angels, who follow Him in the order of causes, leave their imprint on our intellect in so far as we are enlightened, cleansed, and perfected by them, as Dionysius says. But the celestial bodies, which are inferior agents, can leave their imprint only upon our sensible powers and the other powers in our organs. Of course, inasmuch as the movement of one power of the soul flows over into another, it happens that the impression made by a celestial body will, as it were, accidentally flow over into the intellect and finally into the will. Similarly, the impression made by an angel upon our intellect also accidentally flows over into our will.

But the relation of the intellect and of the will to the sensitive powers is different in the following respect: the intellect is naturally moved by the sensitive apprehension in the way in which a potency is moved by an object, because, as is said in *The Soul,* the phantasm is related to the possible intellect as color is to sight. Consequently, whenever an interior sensitive power is disturbed, the intellect is necessarily also disturbed. We see, for example, that when the organ of the imagination is injured the action of the intellect is necessarily impeded. By this means, therefore, the action or influence of a celestial body can flow over into the intel-

lect with a kind of necessity; but this influence
is accidental, because what it directly influences
is the body. I say "necessity" flows over—unless
there is a contrary disposition in what is affected.
But the sensitive appetite is not the natural
mover of the will. Instead, the opposite is true,
because, as is said in *The Soul,* a higher appetite moves a lower "as one sphere" moves another. And no matter how much a lower appetite is troubled by the passion, as of anger
or of concupiscence, the will need not be disturbed. Indeed, the will has the power to repel
a disturbance of this kind; for, as we read in
Genesis (4:7): "The lust thereof shall be under
thee." Consequently, no necessity is introduced
into human acts by the influence of celestial
bodies, either by the celestial bodies themselves
or by those things which receive their influence.
The celestial bodies introduce only an inclination, which the will can resist by means of an
acquired or infused power.

Answers to Difficulties:

1. Damascene is thinking of bodily habits and
dispositions.

2. From what was said above, it is clear that
an act of the will in the soul does not necessarily
follow the disposition of the body. From the
temperament of the body, only an inclination
arises to those things which are the object of the
will.

3. That argument would proceed correctly if a

heavenly body could leave its impression on the essence of the soul directly. But the influence of a heavenly body reaches to the essence of the soul only indirectly, that is, only in so far as the soul is united to a body, whose act the soul is. The will, however, does not have its origin in the essence of the soul in so far as the soul is joined to a body. Consequently, the argument proves nothing.

4. An instrument of a spiritual agent acts through a spiritual power only as it acts through its own material power. Because of its material power, however, a heavenly body can act upon our bodies only. Consequently, the action that arises from its spiritual power can arrive at the soul only indirectly, that is, through the mediation of man's body. However, the material and spiritual power of a heavenly body can influence man's body directly. Because of its material power it moves elementary qualities, such as hot, cold, and so forth; and because of its spiritual power it moves to species and to those effects following the entire species which cannot be reduced to elementary qualities.

5. There are in those bodies some effects of the heavenly bodies which are not caused by heat or cold, such as the attraction of iron by a magnet. In this way some disposition is left in a human body by a celestial body; and by reason of this disposition the soul that is joined to such a body is inclined to this or that craft.

6. If we must "save" the words of Isaac, we

have to understand them to mean merely an inclination in the manner described above.

7. For the most part, a large group follows its natural inclinations, for, as members of a group, men give in to the passions of the group. But by using their intelligence wise men overcome these passions and inclinations. Consequently, it is more probable that a large group will do what a celestial body inclines it to do than that one individual will; for he may use his reason to overcome this inclination. Similarly, if there is a large group of hot-tempered men, it is unlikely that they will not be angered, although it is more likely that an individual will not.

Predestination

ARTICLE I

This Question Treats Predestination. In the First Article We Ask: DOES PREDESTINATION BELONG TO KNOWLEDGE OR WILL?

Difficulties:

It seems that it has will as its genus, for

1. As Augustine says, predestination is the intention of being merciful. But intention belongs to the will. Consequently, predestination also belongs to the will.

2. Predestination seems to be the same as the eternal election referred to in the Epistle to the Ephesians (1:4): "He chose us in him before the foundation of the world"—because the chosen are the same as the predestined. Now, according to the Philosopher, choice belongs rather to appetite than to intellect. Hence, predestination belongs more to the will than to knowledge.

3. But it was said that election comes before predestination and is not the same as it. On the contrary, will comes after knowledge, not before it. But choice pertains to the will. If, therefore,

choice comes before predestination, then predestination cannot belong to knowledge.

4. If predestination belonged to knowledge, then it would seem to be the same as foreknowledge; and thus whoever foreknew the salvation of a person would predestine him. Now, this is false; for the prophets foreknew the salvation of the Gentiles; yet they did not predestine it. Therefore:

5. Predestination implies causality. Now, causality does not have the nature of knowledge, but rather the nature of will. Consequently, predestination belongs more to the will than to knowledge.

6. The will differs from a passive potency in this respect, that the latter refers only to effects taking place in the future, for we cannot speak of passive potency in relation to things that are or have been, whereas the will extends equally to both present and future effects. Now, predestination has both present and future effects; for, as Augustine says: "Predestination is the preparation of grace in the present and of glory in the future." Therefore, it belongs to the will.

7. Knowledge is not related to things in so far as they are made or to be made but in so far as they are known or to be known. Now, predestination is related to a thing as something that must be effected. Consequently, it does not belong to knowledge.

8. An effect receives its name from its proximate cause rather than from its remote cause.

For example, we say that a man is begotten by a man, instead of saying by the sun, which also begets him. Now, preparation is the effect of both knowledge and will, but knowledge is prior to the will and more remote than it. Consequently, preparation belongs more to the will than to knowledge. But, as Augustine says: "Predestination is the preparation of someone for glory." Therefore, predestination pertains rather to the will than to knowledge.

9. When many motions are ordered to only one term, then the entire co-ordinated complex of motions takes the name of the last motion. For example, in the drawing out of a substantial form from the potency of matter, the following order is had: first, alteration, then generation. But the whole is called generation. Now, when something is prepared, this order is had: first, movements of knowledge, then movements of the will. Consequently, the whole should be attributed to the will; therefore, predestination seems to be especially in the will.

10. If one of two contraries is appropriated to something, then the other contrary is removed from it in the highest possible degree. Now, evil is appropriated especially to God's foreknowledge, for we say that the damned are known beforehand. Consequently, His foreknowledge does not have good things as its object. Predestination, however, is concerned only with those good things that lead to salvation. Therefore, predestination is not related to foreknowledge.

11. When a word is used in its proper sense, it does not need a gloss. But whenever the sacred Scripture speaks of knowledge of good, a gloss is added saying that this means approval. This is evident from the *Gloss* on the first Epistle to the Corinthians (8:3): " 'If any man love God, the same is known by him'—that is, he is approved by God"; and from the *Gloss* on the second Epistle to Timothy (2:19): " 'The Lord knoweth who are his'—that is, God approves him." In its proper sense, therefore, knowledge is not related to good things. But predestination is related to good things. Therefore:

12. To prepare belongs to a power that moves, for preparation is related to some work. But, as has been said, predestination is a preparation. Therefore, it belongs to a moving power and so to the will, not to knowledge.

13. A reasoning power modeled upon another reasoning power imitates it. Now, in the case of the human reason, which is modeled upon the divine, we see that preparation belongs to the will, not to knowledge. Consequently, divine preparation is similar; and the conclusion is the same as before.

14. Although the divine attributes are one reality, the difference between them is manifested in the difference in their effects. Consequently, something said of God should be reduced to that attribute to which this effect is appropriated. Now, grace and glory are the effects of predestination, and they are appropriated either to His

will or His goodness. Therefore, predestination also belongs to His will, not to His knowledge.

To the Contrary:

1'. The *Gloss* on the Epistle to the Romans (8::29), "For whom he foreknew, he also predestines," says: "Predestination is God's foreknowledge and preparation of benefits. . . ."

2'. Whatever is predestined is known, but the opposite is not true. Consequently, what is predestined belongs to the class of things that are known; hence, it is included in the genus of knowledge.

3'. A thing should be placed in the genus to which it always belongs, rather than in a genus which is not always proper to it. Now, the element of knowledge always belongs to predestination, because foreknowledge always accompanies it. The granting of grace, however, which takes place through the will, does not always accompany predestination, since predestination is eternal while the bestowal of grace takes place in time. Predestination, therefore, should be placed in the genus of knowledge rather than in that of will acts.

4'. The Philosopher places habits of knowing and doing among the intellectual virtues, for they belong more to reason than to appetite. This is clearly what he does in the case of art and prudence, as can be seen in his *Ethics.* Now, predestination implies a principle of doing and of knowing, since, as is evident from the definition given, predestination is both foreknowledge and preparation. Predestination, therefore, belongs more to knowledge than it does to the will.

5'. Contraries belong to the same genus. But predestination is the contrary of reprobation. Now, since reprobation belongs to the genus of knowledge, because God foreknows the malice of the damned but does not cause it, it seems that predestination also belongs to the genus of knowledge.

R E P L Y :

Destination (from which *predestination* is derived) implies the direction of something to an end. For this reason, one is said to destine a messenger if he directs him to do something. And because we direct our decisions to execution as to an end, we are said to destine what we decide. For example, Eleazar (2 Machabees 6:19) is said to have "destined" in his heart not to do "any unlawful things for the love of life."

Now, the particle *pre-,* when joined to a word, adds a relation to the future. Consequently, *to destine* refers to what is present, while *to predestine* can also refer to what is future. For two reasons, therefore, predestination is placed under providence as one of its parts, namely, because direction to an end, as pointed out in the preceding question, pertains to providence, and because providence—even according to Cicero—includes a relation to the future. In fact, some define providence by saying that it is present knowledge bearing upon future event.

On the other hand, predestination differs from providence in two respects. Providence means a general ordering to an end. Consequently, it extends to all things, rational or irrational, good or bad, that have been ordained by God to an end. Predestination, however, is concerned only with that end which is possible for a rational creature, namely, his eternal glory. Consequently, it concerns only men, and only with reference to those things that are related to salvation. Moreover, predestination differs from providence in a second respect. In any ordering to an end, two things must be considered: the ordering itself, and the outcome or result of the ordering, for not everything that is ordered to an end reaches that end. Providence, therefore, is concerned only with the ordering to the end. Consequently, by God's providence, all men are ordained to beatitude. But predestination is also concerned with the outcome or result of this ordering, and, therefore, it is related only to those who will attain heavenly glory. Hence, providence is related to the initial establishment of an order, and predestination is related to its outcome or result; for the fact that some attain the end that is eternal glory is not due primarily to their own power but to the help of grace given by God.

Therefore, just as we said above that providence consists in an act of reason, like prudence, of which it is a part, because it belongs to reason alone to direct and to ordain, so now we say that predestination also consists in an act of reason, directing or ordering to an end. However, the willing of an end is required before there can be direction to an end, because no one directs anything to an end which he does not will. This is why the Philosopher says that a perfect prudential choice can be made only by a man of good moral character, because moral habits strengthen one's affections for the end which prudence dictates. Now, the one who predestines does not consider in a general way the end to which his predestination directs him; he considers it, rather, according to the relation it has to one who attains it, and such a person must be distinct in the mind of the one predestining from those persons who will not achieve this end. Consequently, predestination presupposes a love by which God wills the salvation of a person. Hence, just as a prudent man directs to an end only in so far as he is temperate or just, so God predestines only in so far as He loves.

Another prerequisite of predestination is the choice by which he who is directed to the end infallibly is separated from others who are not ordained to it in the same manner. This separation, however, is not on account of any difference, found in the predestined, which could arouse God's love; for, as we read in the Epistle to the Romans (9:11-13): "When the children were not yet born nor had done any good or evil

. . . it was said . . . 'Jacob I have loved, but Esau I have hated.' " Consequently, predestination presupposes election and love, and election presupposes love. Again, two things follow upon predestination: the attainment of the end, which is glory, and the granting of help to attain this end, namely, the bestowal of the grace that pertains to the call to be among the predestined. Predestination, therefore, has two effects: grace and glory.

Answers to Difficulties:

1. The acts of the soul are such that a preceding act in some way is virtually contained in the act that follows. Since predestination presupposes love, an act of the will, the notion of predestination includes something that belongs to the will. For this reason, intention and other elements belonging to the will are sometimes put into its definition.

2. Predestination is not the same as election, but, as we said above, it presupposes election. This is why the predestined are the same as the elect.

3. Since choice belongs to the will, and direction to the intellect, direction always precedes election if both have the same object. But if they have different objects, then there is no inconsistency in election's coming before predestination, which implies the existence of direction. As election is taken here, however, it pertains to one who is directed to an end; and the acceptance

of one who is to be directed toward an end comes before the direction itself. In the case stated, therefore, election precedes predestination.

4. Even though predestination is placed under the genus of knowledge, it adds something to knowledge and foreknowledge, namely, direction or an order to an end. In this respect, it resembles prudence, which also adds something to the notion of knowledge. Consequently, just as every person who knows what to do is not thereby prudent, so also not every one who has foreknowledge thereby predestines.

5. Even though causality does not belong to the notion of knowledge as such, it belongs to that knowledge which directs and orders to an end; and direction of this kind is not proper to the will but to the intellect alone. Similarly, understanding does not belong to the nature of a rational animal in so far as it is animal but only in so far as it is rational.

6. Knowledge is related to both present and future effects, just as the will is. On this basis, therefore, it cannot be proved that predestination belongs more to one than to the other. Yet predestination, properly speaking, is related only to the future—as the prefix *pre-* indicates, because it implies an ordering to the future. Nor is it the same to speak of having an effect *in the present* and of having a present effect, because whatever pertains to the state of this life—whether it be present, past, or future—is said to be *in the present.*

7. Even though knowledge as knowledge is not related to things in so far as they are to be made, practical knowledge is related to things under this aspect, and predestination is reduced to this type of knowledge.

8. In its proper sense, preparation implies a disposing of a potency for act. There are, however, two kinds of potencies: active and passive; consequently, there are two kinds of preparations. There is a preparation of the recipient, which we speak of when we say that matter is prepared for a form. Then there is a preparation of the agent, which we speak of when we say that someone is preparing himself in order to do something. It is this latter kind of preparation that predestination implies; for it asserts simply this, that in God there exists the ordering of some person to an end. Now, the proximate principle of ordering is reason, and, as is clear from above, its remote principle is will. Consequently, for the reason given in the difficulty, predestination is attributed more to reason than to will.

9. A similar answer should be given to the ninth difficulty.

10. Evil things are ascribed as proper to foreknowledge, not because they are more proper objects of foreknowledge than good things, but because good things in God imply something more than mere foreknowledge, while evil things have no such added implication. Similarly, a convertible term which does not signify an essence appropriates to itself the name of prop-

erty, which belongs just as properly to the definition, because the definition adds a certain priority.

11. A gloss does not always mean that a word has not been used in its proper sense. Sometimes a gloss is necessary merely to make specific what has been stated in a general way. This is why the gloss explains *knowledge* as meaning knowledge of approval.

12. To prepare or direct belongs only to powers that move. But to move is not peculiar to the will. As is clear from *The Soul,* this is also a property of the practical intellect.

13. In so far as preparation made even in a human reason implies an ordering or directing to an end, it is an act proper to the intellect, not to the will.

14. When treating a divine attribute, we should not consider only its effect but also its relation to the effect; for, while the effects of knowledge, power, and will are the same, still, as the names of these attributes imply, their relations to them are not. Now, in so far as predestination is directive, the relation implied by predestination to its effect is more logically said to be a relation of knowledge than a relation of power or will. Consequently, predestination is reduced to a type of knowledge.

Answers to Contrary Difficulties:

1′.-2′.-4′. We concede the other arguments presented here. One might reply to the second, however, by pointing out that not everything that is found in more things is thereby a genus, for it might be predicated of them as an accident.

3'. Even though the granting of grace does not always accompany predestination, the will to grant grace always does.

5'. Reprobation is directly opposed, not to predestination, but to election, for He who chooses accepts one and rejects another and this is called reprobation. Consequently, as the word itself shows, *reprobation* pertains more to the will. For to reprobate is, as it were, to reject—except that it might be said that to reprobate means the same as to judge unworthy of admittance. However, reprobation is said to belong to God's foreknowledge for this reason, that there is nothing positive on the part of His will that has any relation to sin. He does not will sin as He wills grace. Yet reprobation is said to be a preparation of the punishment which God wills consequent to sin—not antecedent to it.

ARTICLE II

In the Second Article We Ask: Is FOREKNOWLEDGE
OF MERITS THE CAUSE OF OR REASON FOR
PREDESTINATION?

Difficulties:

It seems that it is, for

1. In his gloss on the verse in Romans (9:15),
"I will have mercy on whom I will have mercy,"
Ambrose writes as follows: "I will give mercy to
him who I know will return with his whole heart
to Me after his error. This is to give mercy to
him to whom it should be given, and not to give
it to one to whom it should not. Consequently,
He calls him who He knows will obey, not him
who He knows will disobey." Now, to obey and
to return to God with all one's heart are meritorious; the opposite actions are demeritorious.
Foreknowledge of merit or of demerit is therefore the cause of God's intention of being merciful to some and of excluding others from His
mercy. This is equivalent to predestination and
reprobation.

2. Predestination includes God's will to save
men. It cannot be said that it includes only His
antecedent will, because, according to this will—
as is said in the first Epistle to Timothy (2:4):
"God wills all men to be saved"; hence, it would

follow that all are predestined. It remains, therefore, that predestination includes only His consequent will. Now, "We are the cause," as Damascene says, "of God's consequent will" according as we merit salvation or deserve damnation.
Our merits foreknown by God are therefore the
cause of predestination.

3. Predestination means primarily God's will
with respect to man's salvation. But men's merits
are the cause of their salvation. Moreover, knowledge causes and specifies the act of the will, since
that which moves the will is a desirable thing
which is known. Consequently, foreknowledge
of merits is a cause of predestination, since two
of the things which foreknowledge contains cause
the two things contained in predestination.

4. Reprobation and predestination signify the
divine essence while connoting an effect. There
is no diversity, however, in the divine essence.
Consequently, the difference between predestination and reprobation comes entirely from their
effects. Now, effects are considered as caused by
us. It is due to us, as cause, therefore, that the
predestined are segregated from the reprobate, as
takes place through predestination. Hence, the
same must be said as before.

5. Taken in itself, the sun is in the same relation to all bodies that can be illuminated, even
though all bodies cannot share its light equally.
Similarly, God is equally related to all, even
though all do not participate in His divine goodness in an equal measure, as the saints and

philosophers say so often. Now, since the sun is in the same relation to all bodies, it is not the cause of the difference that we find in these bodies, namely, that some of them are dark and others bright. This is due, rather, to differences in the physical constitution of the bodies which affect their reception of sunlight. Similarly, the reason for this difference, namely, that some reach salvation and others are damned, or that some are predestined while others are rejected, is to be found not in God but in us. Consequently, our original thesis stands.

6. Good communicates itself. It belongs to the highest good, therefore, to communicate itself in the highest possible degree, that is, as much as each and every thing is capable of receiving it. Consequently, if it does not communicate itself to something, this is because that thing is not capable of receiving it. Now, according to the quality of his merits, a person is capable or not capable of receiving the salvation which predestination ordains. Foreknowledge of merits, therefore, is the reason why some are predestined and others are not.

7. Concerning the passage in Numbers (3:12), "I took Levites . . . ," Origen writes: "Jacob, younger by birth, was judged to be the firstborn. Because what they intended to do was in their hearts, and this was clear to God before they were born or did any good or evil, it was said of them: 'Jacob have I loved, Esau have I hated.' " Now, this love, the saints commonly

explain, pertains to Jacob's predestination. Consequently, God's foreknowledge of the intention Jacob was going to have in his heart was the reason for his predestination. Thus, the same must be said as was said previously.

8. Predestination cannot be unjust, since the ways of the Lord are always the ways of mercy and truth. Nor can there be any form of justice between God and men other than distributive justice. There is no place for commutative justice, since God, who needs none of our good things, receives nothing from us. Now, distributive justice rewards unequally only those that are unequal. But the only cause of inequality among men is difference in merit. Therefore, the reason why God predestines one man and not another is that He foreknows their different merits.

9. As mentioned previously, predestination presupposes election. But a choice cannot be reasonable unless there is some reason why one person is to be preferred to another. Now, in the election we are speaking about, there can be no reason for the preference other than merits. Therefore, since God's choice cannot be irrational, His election and, consequently, His predestination also must be caused by His foreknowledge of merits.

10. Commenting on that verse in the Prophecy of Malachias (1:2-3), "I have loved Jacob, but have hated Esau," Augustine says that "the will of God," by which He chose one and rejected the other, "cannot be unjust, for it came from their

hidden merits." But these hidden merits can enter into an intention only in so far as they are foreknown. Consequently, predestination comes from foreknowledge of merits.

11. As the use of grace is related to the final effect of predestination, so the abuse of it is related to the effect of reprobation. Now, in the case of Judas, the abuse of grace was the reason for his reprobation, since he was made reprobate because he died without grace. Moreover, the fact that he did not have grace when he died was not due to God's unwillingness to give it but to his unwillingness to accept it—as both Anselm and Dionysius point out. Consequently, the good use of grace by Peter or anyone else is the reason why he is elected or predestined.

12. One person can merit the first grace for another. For the same reason, it seems that he could merit for that other person a continuation of grace up to the end. Now, if one gets final grace, he is predestined. Consequently, predestination can be caused by merits.

13. According to the Philosopher: "One thing is said to be prior to another when the sequence of their being cannot be reversed." But God's foreknowledge is related to predestination in this way, because God knows beforehand what He predestines, while He foreknows the evil which He does not predestine. Foreknowledge, therefore, is antecedent to predestination. But what is prior in any order is the cause of what is pos-

terior. Consequently, foreknowledge is the cause of predestination.

14. The word *predestination* is derived from *sending* or *destining*. But knowledge precedes sending or destining, because no one can send a person without knowing him first. Knowledge, therefore, is prior also to predestination; hence, it seems that it is the cause of predestination. Consequently, our thesis stands.

To the Contrary:

1'. The *Gloss* on the following verse in the Epistle to the Romans (9:12), "Not of works, but of him that calleth was it said," reads: "He shows that the words 'I have loved Jacob, etc.,' were due neither to any previous nor to any future merits." And the *Gloss* on the verse, "Is there injustice with God?" (9:14), says: "Let no one say that God chooses one man and rejects another because He foresaw future works." Consequently, it does not seem that foreknowledge of merits is the cause of predestination.

2'. Grace is the effect of predestination but the principle of merit. Hence, foreknowledge of merits cannot possibly be the cause of predestination.

3'. In the Epistle to Titus (3:5), the Apostle says: "Not by the works of justice which we have done but according to his mercy. . . ." Predestination of one's salvation, therefore, does not arise from foreknowledge of merits.

4'. If foreknowledge of merits were the cause of predestination, then no one would be predestined who did not merit. But some predestined never merit, as is evidently the case of children. Consequently, foreknowledge of merits is not the cause of predestination.

REPLY:

There is this difference between a cause and an effect—that whatever is the cause of the cause must be the cause of the effect, but the cause of the effect is not necessarily the cause of the cause. It is evident, for example, that the first cause produces its effect through a second cause, and so the second cause, in some way, causes the effect of the first cause, although it is not the cause of the first cause.

Now, we must distinguish two aspects of predestination, the eternal predestination itself and its twofold temporal effect, grace and glory. Glory has human acts as its meritorious cause, but grace cannot have human acts as its meritorious cause; human acts can act only as a certain material disposition to grace, inasmuch as through these acts men are prepared for the acceptance of it. It does not follow from this, however, that our acts, whether they precede or follow grace, are the cause of predestination.

Now, to discover the cause of predestination we must recall what we have said previously, namely, that predestination is a certain direction to an end, and this direction is brought about by reason, moved by the will. Consequently, a thing can be the cause of predestination if it can move the will. However, a thing can move the will in two ways, first, as something due, secondly, as something not due. Now, as something due, a thing can move the will in two ways, namely, either absolutely or on the supposition of something else. The ultimate end, which is the object of the will, moves absolutely; and it moves the will in such a fashion that the will cannot turn away from it. For example, as Augustine says, no man is capable of not willing to be happy. But that without which an end cannot be had is said to move as something due "on the supposition of something else." If an end can be had, however, without a certain thing which contributes merely to the well-being of the end, then that thing does not move the will as something due. In this case, the will inclines to it freely; but when the will is already inclined to it freely, the will is thereby inclined to all the things without which it cannot be had, as to things that are due on the supposition of that which was first willed. For example, out of liberality a king makes a person a soldier; but, because one cannot be a soldier without a horse, on the supposition of the afore-mentioned liberality, giving the soldier a horse becomes due and necessary.

Now, the end-object of the divine will is God's own goodness, which does not depend on anything else. God needs nothing to help Him possess it. Consequently, His will is inclined first to make something freely, not something due, inasmuch as it is His goodness that is manifested in His works. But, supposing that God wishes to make something, it follows as something due from the supposition of His liberality that He make those things also without which those that He has first willed cannot be had. For example, if He wills to make a man, He must give him an intellect. But if there is anything which is not necessary for that which God wills, then that thing comes from God, not as something due, but simply as a result of His generosity. Now, the perfection of grace and glory are goods of this kind, because nature can exist without them inasmuch as they surpass the limits of natural powers. Consequently, the fact that God wishes to give grace and glory is due simply to His generosity. The reason for His willing these things that arise simply from His generosity is the overflowing love of His will for His end-object, in which the perfection of His goodness is found. The cause of predestination, therefore, is nothing other than God's goodness.

According to these principles, a solution can be found to the controversy that has been taking place between certain groups. Some have asserted that everything comes from God's simple pleasure, while others say that everything which comes from God is due. Both opinions are false. The former ignores the necessary order that exists between the things God causes, and the latter asserts that everything arises from God because of a natural necessity. A middle course must therefore be chosen so that it may be laid down that those things which are first willed by God come from His simple pleasure, but those that are required for this first class of things come as something due, although on the basis of a supposition. This "debt" does not, however, make God obliged to things but only to His own will; for what is said to come from God as something due is due simply in order that His will be fulfilled.

Answers to Difficulties:

1. Divine providence ordains that grace bestowed be used as it should. Consequently, it is impossible for foreknowledge of this right use of grace to be the cause that moves God to give grace. The words of Ambrose, "I will give grace to him who I know will return to me with his whole heart," cannot be understood as meaning that a perfect change of heart inclines God's will to give grace but that His will ordains that the grace given be accepted by the person and that he be turned completely toward God.

2. Predestination includes God's consequent will, which is related in some way to that which we cause on our part, not by inclining the divine will to act, but by bringing about that effect for which His will has ordained grace or by bringing about that which, in a certain sense, disposes us for grace and merits glory.

3. While it is true that knowledge moves the

will, not every kind of knowledge does this but only knowledge of an end; and an end is an object moving the will. Consequently, it is because of His knowledge of His own goodness that God loves it; and, from this love, He wishes to pour out His goodness upon others. But it does not therefore follow that knowledge of merits is the cause of His will in so far as it is included in predestination.

4. Although the different formal characters of God's attributes are drawn from the differences in their effects, it does not follow from this that these effects are the cause of His attributes. For the different formal characteristics of His attributes are not derived from our qualities as though our qualities caused them; rather, our qualities are signs that the attributes themselves are causes. Consequently, it does not follow that that which comes from us is the reason why one man is reprobated and another predestined.

5. We can consider God's relation to things in two ways. We can consider it only with respect to the first disposition of things that took place according to His divine wisdom, which established different grades of things. If only this is considered, then God is not related to all things in the same way. We can, however, consider His relation to things also according to the way in which He provides for them as already disposed. If His relation to them is considered in this manner, then He is related to all things in the same way, because He gives equally to all, according

to the proportion He has made. Now, all that
has been said to proceed from God, according to
His will taken simply, belongs to the first disposition of things, of which preparation for grace
is a part.

6. It belongs to the divine goodness as infinite
to give from its perfections whatever the nature
of each thing requires and is capable of receiving.
But this is not required for superabundant perfections such as grace and glory. Hence, the
argument proves nothing.

7. God's foreknowledge of what lay in the
heart of Jacob was not the reason for His willing
to give grace to him. Instead, the intention in
Jacob's heart was a good for which God ordained
the grace to be given to him. It is for this reason
that God is said to have loved him "because his
heart's intention was known by Him." For God
loved him in order that he might have such an
intention in his heart or because He foresaw that
his heart's intention was a disposition for the
acceptance of grace.

8. It would be contrary to the nature of distributive justice if things that were due to persons and were to be distributed to them were
given out unequally to those that had equal
rights. But things given out of liberality do not
come under any form of justice. I may freely
choose to give them to one person and not to
another. Now, grace belongs to this class of
things. Consequently, it is not contrary to the
nature of distributive justice if God intends to

give grace to one person and not to another, and does not consider their unequal merits.

9. The election by which God chooses one man and reprobates another is reasonable. There is no reason why merit must be the reason for His choice, however, since the reason for this is the divine goodness. As Augustine says, moreover, a justifying reason for reprobation [in the present] is the fact of original sin in man—for reprobation in the future, the fact that mere existence gives man no claim to grace. For I can reasonably deny something to a person if it is not due to him.

10. Peter Lombard says that Augustine retracted that statement in a similar passage. But, if it must be sustained, then it should be taken as referring to the effect of reprobation and of predestination, which has a meritorious or disposing cause.

11. God's foreknowledge of this abuse of grace was not the reason why Judas was reprobated, unless we are considering only the consequences of this abuse—though it is true that God denies grace to no one who is willing to accept it. Now, the very fact that we are willing to accept grace comes to us through God's predestination. Hence, our willingness cannot be a cause of predestination.

12. Although merit can be the cause of the effect of predestination, it cannot be the cause of predestination itself.

13. Although that with which the consequent

cannot be interchanged is prior in some way, it does not always follow that it is prior as a cause is said to be prior; for, if this were true, then to be colored would be the cause of being a man. Consequently, it does not follow that foreknowledge is the cause of predestination.

14. The answer to this difficulty is clear from our last response.

ARTICLE III

In the Third Article We Ask: Is PREDESTINATION CERTAIN?

Difficulties:

It seems that it has no certitude, for

1. No cause whose effects can vary can be certain of its effects. But the effects of predestination can vary, for one who is predestined may not attain the effect of his predestination. This is clear from the commentary of Augustine on the words of the Apocalypse (3:11), "Hold fast that which thou hast, that no man take . . . ," in which he says: "If one person will not receive glory unless another loses it, then the number of the elect is certain." Now, from this it seems that one could lose and another receive the crown of glory, which is the effect of predestination.

2. Human affairs fall under God's providence

as things in nature do. But, according to the ordering of God's providence, only those natural effects that are produced necessarily by their causes proceed from them with certainty. Now, since the effect of predestination, man's salvation, arises not necessarily but contingently from its proximate causes, it seems that the ordering of predestination is not certain.

3. If a cause has certitude with respect to some effect, that effect will necessarily follow unless there is something that can resist the power of the agent. For example, dispositions in bodies here below are sometimes found to resist the action of celestial bodies; and, as a consequence, these celestial bodies do not produce their characteristic effects, which they would produce were there not something resisting them. But nothing can resist divine predestination, because, as we read in the Epistle to the Romans (9:19): "Who resisteth his will?" Therefore, if divine predestination is ordered with certitude to its effect, its effect will necessarily be produced.

4. The answer was given that the certitude which predestination has of its effect presupposes the second cause. On the contrary, any certitude based on the supposition of something is not absolute but conditional certitude. For example, it is not certain that the sun will cause a plant to bear fruit unless the generative power of the plant is in a favorable condition; and, because of this, the certitude of the sun's producing this effect presupposes the power of the plant as

though the latter were a second cause. Consequently, if the certitude of divine predestination includes the presupposition of a second cause, that certitude will not be absolute but merely conditional—like the certitude I have that Socrates is moving if he runs, and that he will be saved if he prepares himself. Therefore, God will have no more certitude about those who are to be saved than I have. But this is absurd.

5. We read in Job (34:24): "He shall break in pieces many and innumerable, and shall make others to stand in their stead." In explanation of this passage, Gregory writes: "Some fall from the place of life while others are given it." Now, the place of life is that place to which men are ordained by predestination. Hence, one who is predestined can fall short of the effect of predestination; therefore, predestination is not certain.

6. According to Anselm, predestination has the same kind of truth that a proposition about the future has. But a proposition about the future does not have certain and determinate truth. Such a proposition is open to correction—as is clear from that passage in Aristotle where he says: "One about to walk may not walk." Similarly, therefore, the truth that predestination has does not possess certitude.

7. Sometimes one who is predestined is in mortal sin. This was clearly true of Paul when he was persecuting the Church. Now, he can stay in mortal sin until death or be killed immedi-

ately. If either happens, predestination will not obtain its effect. Therefore, it is possible for predestination not to obtain its effect.

8. But it was said that, when it is stated that one predestined may possibly die in the state of sin, the proposition is taken compositely and so is false; for its subject is taken as simultaneously having the determination *predestined.* But if its subject is taken without this determination, then the proposition is taken in a divided sense and is true. On the contrary, with those forms which cannot be removed from the subject, it does not matter whether a thing is attributed to the subject with those qualifying determinations or without them. For example, taken either way, the following proposition is false: "A black crow can be white." Now, predestination is the kind of form that cannot be removed from the one predestined. In the matter at hand, therefore, there is no room for the afore-mentioned distinction.

9. If what is eternal be joined to what is temporal and contingent, then the whole is temporal and contingent. Thus, it is clear that creation is temporal, even though its notion includes God's eternal essence as well as a temporal effect. The same is true of a divine mission, which implies an eternal procession and a temporal effect. Now, even though predestination implies something eternal, it also implies a temporal effect. Therefore, predestination as a whole is

temporal and contingent and, consequently, does not seem to have certitude.

10. What can be or not be cannot have any certitude. But the fact that God predestines to salvation can be or not be. For just as He can, from all eternity, predestine and not predestine, so even now He can predestine and not predestine, since present, past, and future do not differ in eternity. Consequently, predestination cannot have any certitude.

To the Contrary:

1'. In explanation of that verse in the Epistle to the Romans (8:29), "Whom he foreknew, he also predestined," the *Gloss* says: "Predestination is the foreknowledge and preparation of the benefits of God by which whoever are freed are most certainly freed."

2'. If the truth of a thing is unshakable, it must be certain. But, as Augustine says: "The truth of predestination is unshakable." Therefore, predestination is certain.

3'. Whoever is predestined has this predestination from all eternity. But what exists from all eternity cannot be changed. Predestination, therefore, is unchangeable and, consequently, certain.

4'. As is clear from the *Gloss* mentioned above, predestination includes foreknowledge. But, as Boethius has proved, foreknowledge is certain. Therefore, predestination is also certain.

REPLY:

There are two kinds of certitude: certitude of knowledge and certitude of ordination. Now, certitude of knowledge is had when one's knowledge does not deviate in any way from reality, and, consequently, when it judges about a thing as it is. But because a judgment which will be certain about a thing is had especially from its causes, the word *certitude* has been transferred to the relation that a cause has to its effect; therefore, the relation of a cause to an effect is said to be certain when the cause infallibly produces its effect. Consequently, since God's foreknowledge does not imply, in all cases, a relation of a cause to all the things which are its objects, it is considered to have only the certitude of knowledge. But His predestination adds another element, because it includes not only His foreknowledge but also the relation of a cause to its objects, since predestination is a kind of direction or preparation. Thus, not only the certitude of knowledge, but also the certitude of ordination is contained in predestination. Now we are concerned only with the certitude of predestination; the certitude of knowledge, found also in predestination, has been explained in our investigation of God's knowledge.

It should be known that, since predestination is a particular type of providence, not only its notion adds something to providence, but also its certitude adds something to the certitude of providence. Now, the ordering of providence is found to be certain in two respects. First, it is certain with relation to a particular thing, when God's providence ordains things to some particular end, and they attain that end without failure. This is evident in the motions of celestial spheres and in all things in nature that act necessarily. Second, providence is certain in relation to things in general, but not in particular. For example, we see that the power of beings capable of generation and corruption sometimes falls short of the proper effects to which it has been ordered as its proper ends. Thus, the power that shapes bodies sometimes falls short of forming members completely. Yet, as we saw above when treating providence, these very defects are directed by God to some end. Consequently, nothing can fail to attain the general end of providence, even though it may at times fall short of a particular end.

The ordering of predestination, however, is certain, not only with respect to its general end, but also with respect to a particular and determinate end. For one who is ordained to salvation by predestination never fails to obtain it. Moreover, the ordering of predestination is not certain with reference to a particular end in the way in which the ordering of providence is; for, in providence, the ordering is not certain with respect to a particular end unless the proximate cause necessarily produces its effect. In predestination, however, there is certitude with respect

to an individual end even though the proximate
cause, free choice, does not produce that effect
except in a contingent manner.

Hence, it seems difficult to reconcile the infallibility of predestination with freedom of
choice; for we cannot say that predestination
adds nothing to the certitude of providence except the certitude of foreknowledge, because this
would be to say that God orders one who is
predestined to his salvation as He orders any
other person, with this difference, that, in the
case of the predestined, God knows he will not
fail to be saved. According to this position, one
predestined would not differ in ordination from
one not predestined; he would differ only with
respect to [God's] foreknowledge of the outcome.
Consequently, foreknowledge would be the cause
of predestination, and predestination would not
take place by the choice of Him who predestines.
This, however, is contrary to the authority of the
Scriptures and the sayings of the saints. Thus, the
ordering of predestination has an infallible
certitude of its own—over and above the certitude
of foreknowledge. Nevertheless, the proximate
cause of salvation, free choice, is related to predestination contingently, not necessarily.

This can be considered in the following manner. We find that an ordering is infallible in regard to something in two ways. First, an individual cause necessarily brings about its own
effect because of the ordering of divine providence. Secondly, a single effect may be attained

only as the result of the convergence of many
contingent causes individually capable of failure;
but each one of these causes has been ordained
by God either to bring about that effect itself if
another cause should fail or to prevent that other
cause from failing. We see, for example, that all
the individual members of a species are corruptible. Yet, from the fact that one succeeds
another, the nature of the species can be kept
in existence; and this is how God keeps the
species from extinction, despite the fact that the
individual perishes.

A similar case is had in predestination; for,
even though free choice can fail with respect to
salvation, God prepares so many other helps
for one who is predestined that he either does
not fail at all or, if he does fail, he rises again.
The helps that God gives a man to enable him to
gain salvation are exhortations, the support of
prayer, the gift of grace, and all similar things.
Consequently, if we were to consider salvation
only in relation to its proximate cause, free
choice, salvation would not be certain but contingent; however, in relation to the first cause,
namely, predestination, salvation is certain.

Answers to Difficulties:

1. The word crown as used in the Apocalypse
(3:11) may mean either the crown of present
justice or the crown of future glory. No matter
which meaning is taken, however, one person is
said to receive the crown of another when that

other person falls in the sense that the goods of one person help another, either by aiding him to merit or even by increasing his glory. The reason for this is that all the members of the Church are connected by charity in such a way that their goods are common. Consequently, one receives the crown of another when that other falls through sin and does not achieve the reward of his merits; and another person receives the fruits of the sinner's merits, just as he would have benefited from the sinner's merits had the latter persevered. From this, however, it does not follow that predestination is ever in vain.

Or it can be answered that one is said to receive the crown of another, not because the other lost a crown that was predestined for him, but because whenever a person loses the crown that was due to him because of the justice he possessed, another person is substituted in his place to make up the number of the elect—just as men have been substituted to take the place of the fallen angels.

2. A natural effect issuing infallibly from God's providence takes place because of one proximate cause necessarily ordered to the effect. The ordering of predestination, however, is not made certain in this manner but in the manner described above.

3. A celestial body, taken in itself, imposes a kind of determinism in its action on bodies here below. Consequently, its effect necessarily takes place, unless something resists it. But God does

not act on the will in the manner of one necessitating; for He does not force the will but merely moves it, without taking away its own proper mode, which consists in being free with respect to opposites. Consequently, even though nothing can resist the divine will, our will, like everything else, carries out the divine will according to its own proper mode. Indeed, the divine will has given things their mode of being in order that His will be fulfilled. Therefore, some things fulfill the divine will necessarily, other things, contingently; but that which God wills always takes place.

4. The second cause, which we must suppose as prerequisite for obtaining the effect of predestination, lies also under the ordering of predestination. The relationship between lower powers and the power of a superior agent is not one of predestination. Consequently, even though the ordering of God's predestination includes the supposition of a human will, it nevertheless has absolute certitude, despite the fact that the example given points to the contrary.

5. Those words of Job and Gregory should be referred to the state of present justice. If some fall from it, others are chosen in their place. From this, therefore, we cannot conclude to any uncertainty with reference to predestination; for those who fall from grace at the end were never predestined at all.

6. The comparison Anselm makes holds good in this respect, that just as the truth of a proposi-

tion about the future does not remove con
tingency from a future event, so also the truth
of predestination [does not take away the con
tingency of predestination]. But, in another respect, the comparison is weak. For a proposition
about the future is related to the future in so far
as it is future, and, under this aspect, it cannot
be certain. As we pointed out previously, however, the truth of predestination and foreknowledge is related to the future as present, and, consequently, is certain.

7. A thing can be said to be possible in two
ways. First, we may consider the potency that
exists in the thing itself, as when we say that a
stone can be moved downwards. Or we may consider the potency that exists in another thing,
as when we say that a stone can be moved up-
wards, not by a potency existing in the stone, but
by a potency existing in the one who hurls it.

Consequently, when we say: "That predestined
persons can possibly die in sin," the statement is
true if we consider only the potency that exists
in him. But, if we are speaking of this predestined person according to the ordering which he
has to another, namely, to God, who is predestining him, that event is incompatible with this
ordering, even though it is compatible with the
person's own power. Hence, we can use the distinction given above; that is, we can consider the
subject with this form or without it.

8. Blackness and whiteness are, in a sense, ex-
amples of forms that exist in a subject said to be

white or black. Consequently, nothing can be attributed to the subject, either according to potency or according to act, as long as blackness remains, if it is repugnant to this form of blackness. Predestination, however, is a form that exists, not in the person predestined, but in the one predestining, just as the *known* gets its name from knowledge in the knower. Consequently, no matter how fixed predestination may remain in the order of knowledge, yet, if we consider only the nature [of the predestined], we can attribute something to it which is repugnant to the ordering of predestination. For, considered this way, predestination is something other than the man who is said to be predestined, just as blackness is something other than the essence of a crow, even though it is not something outside the crow, but, by considering only the essence of a crow, one can attribute to it something that is repugnant to its blackness. For this reason, as Porphyry says, one can think of a white crow. Similarly, in the problem being discussed, one can attribute something to a predestined person taken in himself which cannot be attributed to him in so far as he is predestined.

9. Creation and mission imply the production of a temporal effect. Consequently, they affirm the existence of a temporal effect, and so must be temporal themselves, even though they include something eternal. Predestination, however, does not imply the production of a temporal effect—as the word itself shows—but only an

ordering to something temporal, such as will, power, and all such attributes also imply. Since it does not affirm the actual existence of a temporal effect, which is also contingent, predestination is not necessarily temporal and contingent itself, because from eternity something can be unchangeably ordained to a temporal and contingent effect.

10. Absolutely speaking, it is possible for God to predestine or not to predestine each and every person, and it is possible for Him to have predestined or not to have predestined. For, since the act of predestination is measured by eternity, it never is past and never is future. Consequently, it is always considered as issuing from His will as something free. Because of the supposition, however, certain things are impossible: He cannot predestine if He has predestined, and He cannot predestine if He has already not predestined—for God does not change. Hence, it does not follow that predestination can change.

ARTICLE IV

In the Fourth Article We Ask: Is THE NUMBER OF
PREDESTINED CERTAIN?

Difficulties:

It seems not, for

1. No number is certain if something can be
added to it. But something can be added to the
number of the predestined, because Moses' peti-
tion for such an increase is described in Deuteronomy (1:11) where he says: "The Lord God
of your fathers add to this number many thou-
sands." And the Gloss comments: "This number
is fixed by God, who knows who belong to Him."
Now, unless such an addition were possible,
Moses would have asked in vain. Consequently,
the number of the predestined is not certain.

2. As we are prepared for grace through the
disposition of natural prefections, so are we prepared through grace for the attainment of glory.
Now, grace is found in whomsoever there is
sufficient preparation of natural gifts. Similarly,
then, glory will be found wherever grace is found.
But one not predestined may, at one time, possess
grace. Therefore, he will possess glory and so be
predestined. Consequently, one not predestined
may become predestined. In this way, the num-

ber of the predestined can be increased; hence, it is not certain.

3. If one who has grace is not to have glory, his loss of glory will be due to a failure either on the part of grace or on the part of the one giving glory. However, this loss cannot be due to a failure on the part of grace, for, in itself, it sufficiently disposes for glory; nor can it be due to a failure on the part of the one giving glory, for, on His part, He is ready to give it to all. Consequently, whoever has grace will necessarily have glory. Thus, one who is foreknown [as lost] will have glory and be predestined. Accordingly, our original argument stands.

4. Whoever prepares himself sufficiently for grace, gets grace. But one foreknown [as lost] can prepare himself for grace. Therefore, it is possible for him to have grace. Whoever has grace, however, can persevere in it. So it seems that one who is foreknown [as lost] can persevere in grace up to the time of his death and thus become predestined. Consequently, the same must be said as before.

5. It was said, however, that God's foreknowledge that a man will die without grace is necessary by conditional necessity, not by absolute necessity. On the contrary, any necessity which lacks a beginning and an end, and which is without succession, is not conditional but simple and absolute. Now, this is the kind of necessity that the necessity of foreknowledge is, because it is

eternal. Therefore, it is simple and not conditioned.

6. A number larger than any finite number is possible. But the number of the predestined is finite. Therefore, a larger number is possible, and the number of the predestined is not certain.

7. Since good communicates itself, infinite goodness should not impose a limit on its communication. Now, the divine goodness communicates itself to the predestined in the highest possible degree. Therefore, it does not belong to the divine goodness to establish a certain number of predestined.

8. Like the creation of things, the predestination of men depends on the divine will. Now, God can make more things than He has made, because, as we read in Wisdom (12:18): "His power is at hand when He wills." Similarly, He has not predestined so many men that He cannot predestine more; and so our original argument returns.

9. Whatever God was at one time able to do He still is able to do. But from eternity God was able to predestine one whom He did not predestine. Consequently, He is still able to predestine him, and so an addition can be made to the number of the predestined.

10. In the case of all powers not determined to one course of action, what can be can also not be. Now, the power of the one predestining with respect to the one to be predestined, and the

power of the one predestined with respect to his obtaining the effect of predestination, belong to this class of powers, because the one predestining predestines by his will, and the one predestined obtains the effect of predestination by his will. Consequently, the predestined can be non-predestined, and the non-predestined can be predestined. Hence, the conclusion is the same as before.

11. In commentary on that verse in Luke (5:6), "And their net broke," the *Gloss* reads: "In the Church, the net of circumcision is broken, for not as many Jews enter as were preordained by God to life." Consequently, since the number of the predestined can be diminished, it is not certain.

To the Contrary:

1'. Augustine says: "The number of the predestined is certain and can neither be increased nor diminished."

2'. Augustine says: "The heavenly Jerusalem, our mother, the City of God, will not be robbed of any of the number of its citizens nor will it reign with more than the predestined number." Now, the citizens mentioned are the predestined. Consequently, the number of the predestined cannot be increased or decreased. Hence, it is certain.

3'. Whoever is predestined is predestined from eternity. But what exists from eternity is unchangeable, and what did not exist from eternity can never be eternal. Consequently, he who is not predestined cannot be predestined and, conversely, he who is predestined cannot be non-predestined.

4'. After the resurrection, all the predestined will be in the highest heaven with their own bodies. Now, that place is finite, since all bodies are finite, and, as is commonly held, not even two glorified bodies can exist simultaneously [in one place]. Consequently, the number of the predestined should be determinate.

REPLY:

Treating this question, some have distinguished, saying that the number of the predestined is certain if we mean number understood actively or formally, but not certain if we mean number understood passively or materially. For example, one could say that it is certain that one hundred have been predestined, but it is not certain who these one hundred are. The occasion for such a position seems to be the words of Augustine mentioned previously. Augustine seems to imply that one can lose and another receive the predestined crown without the number of the predestined at all varying. But, if those holding this opinion are speaking about certitude of predestination in its relation to the first cause, that is, to God who predestines, then the opinion is entirely absurd, because God Himself has definite knowledge of the number of the predestined, whether the number be taken formally or materially. He knows exactly how many and who are to be saved, and, with respect to both, His ordination is infallible. Consequently, with respect to both numbers, God has certitude, not only of knowledge, but also of ordination.

On the other hand, if we are speaking about the certitude that can be had about the number of the predestined from its relation to the proximate cause of man's salvation (to which predestination is ordained), then our judgment about the formal number and the material number will not be the same. For, since the salvation of each individual has been produced through free choice as through its proximate cause, in some way the material number is subject to man's will, which is changeable. Consequently, the material number in some way lacks certainty. But the formal number is not determined in any manner by man's will, because by no kind of causality does the human will affect the number of the predestined taken as a whole. Consequently, the formal number remains completely certain. In this way the aforementioned distinction can be sustained, as long as we concede, without any qualifications, that both numbers are certain as far as God is concerned.

It should be noted, moreover, that the number of the predestined is certain in this respect, that it cannot be increased or diminished. The number could be increased if one who was foreknown [as lost] could be predestined; but this would be contrary to the certainty of foreknowledge or of reprobation. Again, the number could be diminished if it were possible for one who is predestined to become non-predestined; but this would be contrary to the certainty of predestination. Thus, it is clear that the certitude about the number of the predestined is made up of two certitudes, and certitude of predestination and the certitude of foreknowledge or reprobation. These two certitudes differ, however; for, as has been said, the certitude of predestination is the certitude of knowledge and of direction to an end, while the certitude of foreknowledge is merely the certitude of knowledge. For God does not preordain the reprobate to sin as He ordains the predestined to merit.

Answers to Difficulties:

1. That quotation from Deuteronomy should be understood as referring, not to the number of the predestined, but to the number of those who are in the state of present justice. This is clear from the *Interlinear Gloss,* which adds: "In number and in merit." Now, this number of those in present justice is both increased and diminished; but God's appointment, which predefines this number, too, is never wrong, because it is He who decrees that there be more of these at one time and fewer at another. Or we could even answer that God defines a certain number in the manner of a judgment in harmony with inferior reasons, and this limitation can be changed; but He predestines another number in

the manner of an election in harmony with superior reasons, and this limitation cannot be changed. For Gregory says: "He changes His judgment but never His election."

2. No preparation disposes anything to have a perfection at a time other than its proper time. For example, his natural temperament may dispose a boy to be brave or wise—not, however, in the days of his childhood, but in the days of his manhood. Now, the time when one obtains grace is simultaneous with the time when nature is prepared. Consequently, no barrier can come between them. Thus, when the preparation of nature is found in a person, grace is also found in him. But the time when one obtains glory is not simultaneous with the time when he has grace. Consequently, a barrier can come between these two. For this reason, one who is foreknown to possess grace will not necessarily possess glory also.

3. That one who had grace is nevertheless deprived of glory is not due to failure either on the part of grace or on the part of Him who gives glory. It is due rather to a failure on the part of the recipient, in whom an impediment has arisen.

4. When we affirm that a person is foreknown [as lost], we thereby affirm that he will not have final grace; for, as we pointed out previously, God's knowledge is directed to future things as though they were present. Consequently, just as the condition of not having final grace cannot be reconciled with the condition of having final

grace even though the former condition is possible if taken by itself, so the condition of having final grace cannot be reconciled with the condition of being foreknown [as lost], even though the former condition is also possible if taken by itself.

5. The fact that such a thing known by God is not absolutely necessary comes, not from a defect in God's knowledge, but from a defect in the proximate cause. On the other hand, the reason why this necessity is eternal—without beginning and end, and, as it were, without succession—comes from God's knowledge, which is eternal, not from the proximate cause, which is temporal and changeable.

6. Even though finite number as finite number does not prevent a larger number from existing, the impossibility may come from another source, namely, from the fixed character of God's foreknowledge, which is apparent in the problem at hand. Similarly, when we consider the size of some natural thing, we see that a larger size cannot exist, not because of the nature of quantity, but because of the nature of the thing itself.

7. The divine goodness communicates itself only under the guidance of wisdom, for this is the best manner for its communication. Now, as we read in Wisdom (11:21), the ordering of God's wisdom requires that all things be made according to "number, weight, and measure." Consequently, that there be a definite number of predestined is in harmony with God's goodness.

8. As is clear from what was said previously, while it may be granted with reference to a determined person that God, absolutely speaking, can predestine or not predestine him, nevertheless, supposing that God has predestined him, He cannot not predestine him. Nor is the opposite possible, because God cannot change. Consequently, it is commonly said that the following proposition, "God can predestine one who is not predestined or not predestine one who is predestined," is false if taken in a composite sense, but true if taken in a divided sense. All statements, therefore, which imply that composite sense are absolutely false. Thus, we must not concede that the number of the predestined can be increased or diminished, because addition presupposes something which is increased, and subtraction, something which is diminished. For the same reason, we cannot concede that God can predestine more or fewer than He has already predestined.

Furthermore, the example drawn from the making of things is not to the point; for making is a particular action terminating exteriorly in an effect, and the fact that God makes something first and does not make it later indicates no change in God but only in the effect. On the other hand, predestination, foreknowledge, and similar things are acts intrinsic to God; and no change can take place in them without a change taking place in God. Nothing, therefore, that implies a change in these acts should be granted.

9-10. The answer to these arguments is clear, for they are based on an understanding of God's power as absolute, not as modified by a supposition of predestination or non-predestination.

11. That *Gloss* should be understood as meaning this: the number of Jews entering is not as large as the total number of all those who have been preordained to life, for it is not only Jews who have been predestined. Or one could reply that the *Gloss* is not speaking about the preordination of predestination but about the preordination of preparation by which the Jews were disposed for life by means of the Law. Or, finally, one could reply that not as many Jews entered the early Church as are predestined, because, as we read in the Epistle to the Romans (11:25-26): "When the fulness of the Gentiles should come in . . . all Israel will be saved" in the Church at the end of time.

ARTICLE V

In the Fifth Article We Ask: ARE THE PREDESTINED CERTAIN OF THEIR PREDESTINATION?

Difficulties:

It seems that they are, for

1. The words of St. John, "His unction teacheth you of all things," (1 John 2:27), are under-

stood as referring to all things pertaining to salvation. But predestination pertains very much to salvation, since it is the cause of salvation. Consequently, through an unction they receive, all men are made certain of their predestination.

2. It is consonant with God's goodness, which does all things in the best possible way, to lead men to their reward in the best possible way. Now, the best possible way seems to be that each and every man be certain of his reward. Therefore, each and every person who is predestined is given assurance that he will come to his reward. Consequently, the same must be said as before.

3. All whom the leader of an army enrolls for merit in battle are likewise enrolled for a reward. Consequently, they are as certain about their reward as they are about their merit. But men are certain that they are in the state of meriting. Consequently, they are also certain that they will obtain their reward. We conclude as before.

To the Contrary:

In Ecclesiastes (9:1) we read: "Man knoweth not whether he be worthy of love or hatred."

REPLY:

There is nothing inconsistent in the revelation to some person of the fact of his predestination; but, in view of His general law, it would be inconsistent if He revealed this to all the predestined for the following two reasons. The first reason may be found by considering those who are not predestined. Now, if all the predestined knew that they were predestined, then all those not predestined would know that they were not predestined from the very fact that they did not know if they were predestined. This would, in some way, lead them to despair. The second reason may be found by considering those who are predestined. Now, security is the mother of negligence; and if the predestined were certain about their predestination, they would be secure about their salvation. Consequently, they would not exercise so great care in avoiding evil. Hence, it has been wisely ordained by God's providence that men should be ignorant of their predestination or reprobation.

Answers to Difficulties:

1. When Scripture says that His unction teaches everything connected with salvation, this should be understood as referring to those things knowledge of which pertains to salvation, not to all those things which, in themselves, do pertain to salvation. And, although predestination itself is necessary for salvation, knowledge of predestination is not.

2. It is not proper, when giving a reward, to give the person who is to receive it unconditional assurance. The proper way is to give conditional assurance to the one for whom the reward is being prepared, namely, that the reward will be given him unless he fails on his part. This kind

of assurance is given to all the predestined through the infusion of the virtue of hope.

3. One cannot know with any certainty that he is in the state of meriting, although he can know, by conjecture, that this is probably the case. For a habit never can be known except through its acts, and the acts of the infused supernatural virtues greatly resemble the acts of the acquired natural virtues. Consequently, it is not easy to be certain that acts of this kind have their source in grace, unless, by a special privilege, a person is made certain of it through a revelation. Moreover, he who is enrolled by the leader of an army for a secular struggle is given only conditional assurance of his reward, because one "is not crowned, except he strive lawfully" (2 Timothy 2:5).

ARTICLE VI

In the Sixth Article We Ask: CAN PREDESTINATION BE HELPED BY THE PRAYERS OF THE SAINTS?

Difficulties:

It seems not, for

1. What can be aided can be prevented, but predestination cannot be prevented. Therefore, it cannot be aided in any way.

2. When one thing has its effect whether an-

other thing is present or not, the latter is no help to it. But predestination must have its effect, because it cannot fail whether prayers take place or not. Consequently, predestination is not helped by prayers.

3. Nothing eternal is preceded by something temporal. But prayer is temporal, and predestination is eternal. Therefore, prayer cannot precede predestination, and, consequently, cannot help it.

4. As is clear from the first Epistle to the Corinthians (12:12), the members of the mystical body resemble the members of a natural body. Now, in a natural body, a member does not acquire its perfection by means of another member. Consequently, the same is true [of members] in the mystical body. But the members of the mystical body receive their greatest perfection through the effects of predestination. Therefore, one man is not aided in obtaining the effects of predestination by the prayers of another.

To the Contrary:

1'. We read in Genesis (25:21): "Isaac besought the Lord for his wife because she was barren; and he heard him, and made Rebecca to conceive." As a result of this conception Jacob was born, who had been predestined from all eternity; and this predestination would never have been fulfilled had he not been born. But it was affected by the prayer of Isaac. Consequently, predestination is helped by prayers.

2'. In a certain sermon on the conversion of

St. Paul, in which the Lord is represented as speaking to Paul, we read: "Unless Stephen, my servant, had prayed for you, I would have destroyed you." The prayers of Stephen, therefore, freed Paul from reprobation; and so through these prayers he was predestined. Hence, we conclude as before.

3'. One can merit the first grace for someone. For the same reason, therefore, he can also merit final grace for him. But whoever possesses final grace is predestined. Therefore, the predestination of one person can be furthered by the prayers of another.

4'. As Damascene tells us in a certain sermon on the dead, Gregory prayed for Trajan and freed him from hell. It seems, therefore, that he was freed from the company of the damned by Gregory's prayers. Hence the same must be said as before.

5'. The members of the mystical body resemble the members of a natural body. But in a natural body one member is helped by another. Consequently, the same is true in the mystical body, and the above proposition stands.

REPLY:

That predestination can be helped by the prayers of the saints can be understood in two ways. First, it can mean that the prayers of the saints help one to be predestined. This, however, cannot be true of prayers, either as they exist in their own proper condition, which is temporal while predestination is eternal, or as they exist in God's foreknowledge, because, as explained above, foreknowledge of merits is not the cause of predestination, whether the merits be one's own or those of another. On the other hand, that predestination is furthered by the prayers of the saints can mean that their prayers help us obtain the effect of predestination as an instrument helps one in finishing his work. The problem has been considered in this way by all those who have studied God's providence over human affairs. Their answers, however, have been different.

Attending only to the immutability of God's decrees, some have declared that prayer, sacrifice, and similar actions help in no way at all. This is said to have been the opinion of the Epicureans, who taught that all things happened necessarily because of the influence of celestial bodies, which they called gods.

Others said that sacrifices and prayers help to this extent, that they change the preordination made by those who have the power to determine human acts. This is said to have been the opinion of the Stoics, who taught that all things are ruled by certain spirits whom they called gods; and, even though something had been pre-established by them, according to the Stoics, such a prearrangement could be changed by placating their souls through prayers and sacrifices, Avicenna seems to have fallen into this error, too; for he asserts that all human actions whose principle is the human will can be reduced to the wills of celestial souls. He thought that the heavenly bodies had souls, and, just as a heavenly body influences a human body, so, according to him, the celestial souls influence human souls. In fact, what takes place in things here below is according to the notions of these celestial souls. Consequently, he thought that sacrifices and prayers helped these souls to conceive what we wished to take place.

These theories, however, are opposed to the Faith. For the first destroys freedom of choice; the second, the certainty of predestination. Consequently, we must answer the problem differently, and must say that, while God's predestination never changes, prayers and other good works are nevertheless effective in obtaining the effect of predestination. Now, when considering any order of causes, we must consider not only the order of the first cause to the effect but also the order of the second cause to the effect and the order of the first cause to the second cause, since the second cause is ordered to an effect only through the direction of the first cause. For, as is clear from *The Causes,* the first cause gives to the second cause the power of influencing the effect.

I say, therefore, that the effect of predestination is man's salvation, and this comes from it as from its first cause. It can have, however, many other proximate and, as it were, instrumental causes, which are ordered by divine predestination for man's salvation, as tools are used by a craftsman for completing a product of his craft. Consequently, the effect of God's predestination is not only that an individual person be saved but also that he be saved by certain prayers or certain merits. Gregory also said this: "What holy men effect by their prayers is predestined to be obtained by prayer." Consequently, Boethius says: "If we pray well, our prayers cannot be without effect."

Answers to Difficulties:

1. There is nothing that can check the ordering of predestination. Consequently, predestination cannot be impeded. Many things, however, are related to the ordering of predestination as intermediate causes; and these are said to further predestination in the manner described.

2. From the fact that it is predestined that a certain man will be saved because of certain prayers, these prayers cannot be omitted without detriment to his predestination. The same is true of man's salvation, which is the effect of predestination.

3. The argument proves that prayer does not help predestination by being, as it were, its cause. This we concede.

4. The effects of predestination, which are grace and glory, are not, as it were, basic perfections but secondary perfections. Now, even though the members of a natural body do not help each other in acquiring their basic perfec-

tions, they nevertheless do help each other to acquire their secondary perfections. There is, moreover, a member in the body which, having been formed first, helps in the formation of other members—namely, the heart. Consequently, the argument proceeds on a false assumption.

Answers to Contrary Difficulties:

1'. We concede this argument.

2'. Paul was never reprobated according to the disposition made by divine election, because this is unchangeable. He was reprobated, however, according to a [provisional] judgment of God in harmony with lower causes, a judgment which sometimes changes. It follows, therefore, not that prayer was the cause of predestination, but that it furthered only the effect of predestination.

3'. Although predestination and final grace are interchangeable, it does not necessarily follow that whatever is the cause of final grace in any manner whatsoever is also the cause of predestination. This is clear from what has been said previously.

4'. Although Trajan was in the place of the damned, he was not damned absolutely; for he was predestined to be saved by the prayers of Gregory.

5'. We concede the fifth argument.